OUR BETTER SELVES

A Journey of Love Amid Life's Storms

Jan Lovell

WESTBOW
PRESS®
A DIVISION OF THOMAS NELSON
& ZONDERVAN

WestBow Press books may be ordered through booksellers or by contacting:

WestBow Press
A Division of Thomas Nelson & Zondervan
1663 Liberty Drive
Bloomington, IN 47403
www.westbowpress.com
844-714-3454

Scripture quotations taken from The Holy Bible, New International
Version® NIV® Copyright © 1973 1978 1984 2011 by Biblica,
Inc. TM. Used by permission. All rights reserved worldwide.

ISBN: 978-1-6642-8902-4 (sc)
ISBN: 978-1-6642-8904-8 (hc)
ISBN: 978-1-6642-8903-1 (e)

Library of Congress Control Number: 2023900344

Printed in the United States of America.

WestBow Press rev. date: 08/22/2023

Acknowledgements

Many thanks to everyone who shared their stories, for my courageous sister Sue, to Pastor Harlan Seri, and to Tom and Chris for their loving support.

Contents

Introduction

The little girl stretched on her tippy toes at the kitchen sink, grasping to reach the small faucet handles.

She desperately needed that glass of water. Her face was flushed, her ponytail a mess, and she was hot and thirsty after playing tag and jumping rope with her cousins. They always raced to the bottom of her grandma's hillside to play hopscotch on the rutted sidewalk. Playing with her cousins before the university football game was such fun.

She almost reached the handle when she sensed a grown-up approach. It was her Aunt Gladys. She was the aunt whose coiffed hair retained its perfection even in a gale-force wind. Aunt Gladys always wore a tailored pantsuit, not a team sweatshirt, to the big game. She gingerly clapped for touchdowns while the rest of us shrieked, high-fived, and jumped up and down.

But back to the glass of water. "There you are, dear," Aunt Gladys said after filling the glass, handing the little girl the water, and quickly controlling the conversation. "Have you heard? Your older cousin, my eldest son, plans to attend law school. And my youngest son, maybe just two years older than you, plans to become a doctor. What do you want to be when you grow up, dear?"

The little girl gulped water to fill the void. She stared at the floor, debating whether to share her ideas. Then, thankfully, she noticed an untied shoelace on her Red Ball Jets sneaker and bent down to tie it.

"You better be thinking about it," Aunt Gladys warned before returning to the grown-ups. "It is a big decision."

Okay. So that little girl was me. I decided not to share my ideas. What if she laughed at them?

A superhero, a veterinarian, and an Olympic athlete were just a few options on my list of what I wanted to be when I grew up. The possibilities seemed limitless. Just imagine—a job where I could rescue people in the nick of time, help heal a family's beloved pet, or represent our country as among the fastest runners in the world.

Or maybe I'll become a ballerina, I daydreamed after being mesmerized by the magnificent music and graceful dancers who effortlessly swept across the stage in *The Nutcracker* ballet …

My childhood dance instructor, however, helped me come to grips with the reality that Arabesque movements may not be in my genes. Then I found out that veterinarians must give shots to cuddly pets, and winning the fifty-yard dash in sixth grade wasn't quite good enough to qualify for the Olympics. Plus, I never did figure out my unique superpower.

"What do you want to be when you grow up?" we were all continually asked by our teachers, counselors, and relatives. Perhaps you determined your road map when you were young, got on the fast track with your focused education, and quickly reached your lifework destination. Done. Time for the cruise control. Or maybe your road map included taking a detour along a dusty and rutted dirt road, eventually arriving at an unexpected career destination.

I was one of those who cheerfully hoped that my path would unfold as planned if I set goals and worked hard. As a little girl heading into the Sunday school classroom, I loved to stop and gaze at the picture of Jesus surrounded by children from all over the world. His face shone with kindness and love as He helped everyone along a path that wound into the distance. I felt the assurance of His companionship. I did not notice the rugged mountains or storm clouds in the far distance.

But life is what happens when we are busy making plans. And each of us will face storms. Whether it is a loved one or a dear friend who passes away, addiction, disease, a tragic accident, or a global pandemic, we all share the common denominator of having times of hardship.

That is apparently why many perceptive folks throughout the centuries have compared life to riding in a rickety boat on a stormy sea, clinging tightly with fear, hoping for safe passage. "We men and women are all in the same boat, upon a stormy sea" (G. K. Chesterton, volume 28, Oct. 2, 1909).

I don't know about you, but I would like to know how to swim or at least be aware of where the life jackets are if we all will be in this rickety boat at some point in our lives. Some type of guidance or instruction manual would be helpful so that we not only survive the storm but become more resilient.

We have all heard that the challenges in life and how we face them define who we are. But more importantly, those experiences can help shape who we are *becoming*. Instead of focusing on life as a race to reach a career pinnacle when we are "grown-ups," what if the focus was the journey itself? If the journey matters, we can make time to help others along the way and savor our relationships with family and loved ones.

Our goals can include becoming a better person instead of the best.

I was glad to read a national poll a few years ago that resulted in a majority of respondents saying that "being a better person" was their New Year's resolution instead of the usual priorities of "lose weight" and "exercise more." Now *that* is a headline. Rather than the typical self-centered physical goal of looking better, most of those surveyed wanted to behave better with one another.

Our world sorely needs a lot more of us seeking "betterness." We are in a time when a 280-character tweet online can shatter a reputation. Teenagers and elementary school children fear they may be the next shooting rampage victim. The number of hate groups in the United States has risen explosively. Opioid addiction has shattered our life expectancy. Mass killings continue to escalate at any locale—concerts, movie theaters, churches, synagogues, and schools. We have seen lies spread across social media faster than a prairie fire during a drought. Strangers spew anger publicly at other strangers. Polarized political extremes have impeded progress in the halls of Congress and chilled family conversation at the dinner table. Natural disasters are more frequent and severe. Racial tension has erupted. Houses of worship have become targets. Even the United Nations Secretary-General Antonio Guterres sounded a global alarm, "Our world is in peril—and paralyzed."

The distressing news and chaotic distractions can numb us and let what seems like an angry world harden our hearts.

Or, we can listen to our hearts and get off the sidelines. We can choose loving, not hateful, actions. We can look for the lights in the darkness, look for the best in people, be kind and caring, and help leave the world a better place.

It starts with each of us. It is a choice we can ponder while reading the following stories of "ordinary" people faced with life storms that could have swamped their rickety boats. But instead, they chose to live with fullness, intention, resilience, faith, and love. They found their way to being better, not bitter. They went *through* their storms, not around them, to avoid the pain, teaching us all. Their stories and others provide impactful and pragmatic steps to create a My Better Self fitness plan.

A friend told me about her excruciating experiences in her early twenties, including domestic abuse, divorce, and depression. "It's not what we face," said this woman who was a manager in a respected organization. "Everyone has problems. It is who we become as we go through them. And what we have learned when we get to the other side."

Who am I to be telling these stories? I am just a former newspaper reporter. I don't have a psychology, counseling, or seminary degree. However, I have known the searing pain of having a sister die of stage 4 cancer and watching Alzheimer's disease rob my father of precious memories and his intellect. And, against my better judgement, I included some of my own stories so others could learn from my mistakes and shortcomings. It is imperfect, for sure. But so am I.

One story is about my sister Sue, who chose to live life to the fullest even though she was physically dying from cancer. Amid the indescribable pain of not having a cure, Sue helped teach each of us that we could be renewed and restored. We can love and be loved. We can embrace each day and live it with more compassion, purpose, and joy.

I promised my sister I would try to live each day more lovingly and thoughtfully. Gratefully and most importantly, I have learned that I don't have to do it alone. That little girl thirsted for water from the faucet, but He can quench our thirst at any age and time.

PART I

Their Stories

Mary

Rachel was one of those natural athletes. Whether it was volleyball, basketball, or soccer, she enjoyed team sports. But like many thirteen-year-olds, she also liked listening to music, reading and hanging out with friends. Another constant companion was her dog, Max, who was the regular beneficiary of hefty portions of Rachel's meals at the kitchen table.

Rachel relished being outdoors and exploring the rolling prairie woods and the pond near her house in Mantorville, Minnesota. Mantorville was a community of about 1,200 residents near Rochester, Minnesota, and home to the world-famous Mayo Clinic. The wildlife and natural beauty along the Zumbro River provided inspiration and subjects for her to paint with watercolors.

"She enjoyed life," her mom, Mary, said. "She was a typical thirteen-year-old girl on her way to becoming a young woman."

Then the merciless bullying began.

And later, a phone call shattered Mary's world.

It just could not be possible. Mary's daughter, her happy, smiley kid, was in the hospital on life support. Rachel had tried to kill herself.

Rachel did not survive the night. Her untimely death sent ripples throughout Minnesota that are reverberating still today. It sent many loved ones and friends into a tailspin.

Rachel Ehmke had "a beautiful smile and a precocious spark in her big brown eyes," her obituary read. "She was shy to those she didn't know and outgoing, kind, and funny to those who knew her best."

The bullying began with some members of her basketball team who did name-calling in the hallways. It then turned into disparaging remarks on social media that all of her classmates could see. Rachel tried to ignore it, hoping they would tire of it. But it went on for months. Like many teenagers, Rachel didn't want her parents to say anything because that might make it worse. Then someone stuck chewing gum in her textbooks. Rachel and a friend started eating lunch in the locker room to avoid the taunts.

The bullying escalated into public name-calling.

Mary tried talking with some of the girls' moms. One was incredulous that her daughter would do such a thing; another mom had so many family issues that she could not discipline her daughter. Unfortunately, the principal was slow in responding. When he finally talked with the bullying girls, there were no consequences. The school staff was even slow about cleaning Rachel's locker.

Rachel repeatedly told her family that she was fine. Then a few days before her death, somebody sent an anonymous text to several students. The text referred to Rachel with a disparaging label and suggested that students forward it to others to hound her out of school. Mary, who was out of town then, told her daughter they would find out who had pulled this latest horrendous stunt when she got home.

Rachel planned to hang out with her older brother, Jonathan, that weekend but asked him to drop her off at her mom's house so she could do some homework first. Afterward, Jonathan's plans changed, so he asked their dad, Rick, to pick her up.

Rick walked to the front door, but it was locked. He peered through a window and saw his daughter hanging by a noose from a ceiling rafter. He smashed the windows to get inside. She was still breathing. He frantically called 911. Paramedics arrived and took Rachel to the hospital.

Mary started receiving phone calls. She assumed they were more calls from her sixteen-year-old son, Jonathan, who kept pleading with her to unground him from using his PlayStation. So Mary ignored the calls for a while. When she did answer, it was Rick. "I just collapsed."

It was a blur after that, trying to catch a flight home. Other family members were at Rachel's side at the hospital. Doctors told the family around midnight or 1:00 a.m. that Rachel had sustained too much damage to recover. The family asked that she stay on life support so her mom could see her. When Mary rushed into the hospital, it was too late. Her thirteen-year-old daughter's heart had stopped at about 3:00 a.m.

There was an outpouring of community support. The funeral staff eventually had to close the doors at the visitation to give the family rest. More than 1,500 people attended the funeral.

They could have pressed charges, but "they were kids being kids," Mary said. Kids can do hurtful things at that age. "That's not to say they shouldn't have consequences for their actions; they should. The consequences today are the guilt they probably feel.

"It was, ultimately, Rachel's decision. But it's so tough when kids are that age," Mary said. As a doctor told her, their brains are not developed enough at that age to always reconcile immediate social pressures with a positive future. "They can't see beyond here," she said, holding her open palm in front of her face. "They don't think beyond here."

Rachel was an easy target. She did not fight back. Rachel's parents had told her to ignore the bullying. "Maybe I should have told her to fight back." But that was not how they wanted to raise their children.

No one had any idea that Rachel would take such an extreme action. "It was such a shock, such a total shock." Even to her best friend, who didn't have a clue.

That is one of the reasons Mary thinks it was a rash decision—Rachel hadn't planned her suicide. There was no suicide note.

Instead, they found items like a list of what Rachel wanted to do when they went up north to the lake during summer vacation.

Following an investigation, law enforcement officials decided they would not file criminal charges. "While harassment and bullying were likely factors in the seventh grader's death, there is not one incident or action done by any particular student that we believe is responsible for Rachel's death," the local sheriff's department reported. Ultimately, officials determined that Rachel had sent that last text about leaving the school district because she felt she needed to move. And then she got scared people would find out.

How does a parent deal with this grief, this profound tragedy? How do they deal with the second-guessing, the what-ifs, the guilt, and the constant question of *why?*

"I have a very strong faith in God," Mary said without hesitation. "That faith is what got me back on track when I got off."

Rachel didn't die because it was God's plan, as some have said when trying to offer sympathy. "I don't believe God planned this—it happens. We still have self-will."

"It is my understanding that when I was crying, God was crying with me.

"There was a time that I thought I was never going to feel better. The grief was so debilitating." The first year was one of survival. Mary said she never seriously thought of killing herself, but the intense grief could be unbearable. And then she would take a deep breath and another step.

She would lie in Rachel's bed, hoping to once again experience Rachel's scent on her pillow. She would tell Rachel over and over that she loved her.

At this point, Mary stopped talking, shifted in her chair, and looked away. "Okay, I'll tell you this story. It's an important story," she said.

In the weeks after Rachel died, Mary walked down to the pond by their house each day, fervently seeking a connection with her daughter. Rachel loved exploring the nearby woods, especially that pond, where she spent countless hours trying to catch tadpoles or make a haven for ants.

Mary went there because Rachel loved it. Day after day, Mary sat at the end of their small dock. "I would be crying and yelling at God." Then one day, she said to God, "If Rachel is okay, show me something."

Within moments, a turtle came out of the water and swam toward her. It stopped by her feet and paddled close by for several minutes. Time stood still. Then it disappeared. There were other pond critters, but no one had ever seen a turtle in that pond in all those years.

Mary noted that there are many stories of other people who have had creatures appear to them as a sign of comfort from heaven. But typical stories involve pretty creatures like butterflies or birds or soft, fluffy animals—not reptiles, Mary said with a smile. Yet it makes sense that a turtle would have made its first appearance that day. Rachel had loved that pond and all the creatures it sustained.

From that point on, Mary had peace knowing Rachel was okay.

"And isn't that what every parent wants to know—that their child is safe and okay?"

Even with small reassurances, the surviving family of a suicide victim must learn to find their way.

Why? Why did Rachel do this? Why did this happen? Questions plagued Mary over and over for at least the first three years. "There was never an answer."

She talked with the clergy. She spoke with doctors. She met with psychologists. She read feverishly—books about people who suffered painful tragedies and somehow made it through, books about people who found hope even while imprisoned in a Nazi concentration camp.

Alcohol became a way to dull the pain. After about four months, she fell apart. She knew she needed professional help. "I kept coming back to 'Where is God in all of this?'"

She learned at a treatment center that she must embrace the first step of the twelve steps in Alcoholics Anonymous; Mary had to admit she was powerless not only over alcohol but also life in general, as we all are. As president of an independent telecommunications service provider, she was used to being in control. It was her job to determine priorities and who could get them done. The workplace might work that way, but life does not. "We may try to hang on so tight and control everything ..." Mary discovered how critical it is for everyone to learn to surrender.

"People would tell me that I was so strong." But Mary said the road to recovery was to acknowledge weakness, surrender, and realize "that I can't do it alone."

She learned to discipline her mind to focus on staying in gratitude instead of slipping into what she had lost. That meant not just thinking about everything she was thankful for but taking the physical action of writing down a list of all those things and then reading it. And rereading it.

There was the hard work of surrendering. There was the hard work of staying grateful. And there was the hard work of forgiveness.

"We have a choice. We can stay angry and bitter." Or we can choose hope.

Raising Awareness

Rachel's story woke up a lot of people. School leaders reviewed policies, and community awareness increased about the impact of bullying on kids. "Or at least I would like to think so," Mary said softly. "That helps give her death some meaning."

Even amid their grief, Mary and Rick felt it was immediately imperative to spread the message about the destructive power of bullying so no other family had to experience what they had. "She couldn't realize this could be handled, that she could move on," a tearful Mary said when interviewed by a TV reporter within days after Rachel passed away. Rachel had big goals and dreams that will never be fulfilled, Rick said, grasping her photo in his hand. "That keyboard has the power to kill, and it did," Rick said. "It killed my daughter."

As the community became aware Rachel had been bullied, some of the bullies, and others who had not been involved, became targets of teenager scorn. "We want this to stop," Mary said. "Even the kids who were bullying her, don't bully them. This must stop *now*.

"If Rachel's death can somehow save another child, we need to do that."

In the ensuing weeks, Rachel's older sister Brittney and brother Derek spoke at public meetings to raise awareness about the impact of bullying. "I would never wish anything bad upon them or upon their family. And I know my little sister would never want that either ..." What would make a difference? If adults enforced consequences against kids who bully. "Maybe sometime down the road people will see that it didn't have to happen."

Residents tied big purple ribbons around trees on busy streets in both communities. "Stop Bullying" banners lined the main thoroughfares. Hundreds wore white T-shirts with purple lettering that said, "Stop Bullying." Purple was Rachel's favorite color. Volunteers placed donation buckets in local businesses. In addition, community members held a Stop Bullying memorial walk to raise awareness and funds.

Local and statewide media covered her tragic death in 2012. Students expressed their heartache on social media. A hip-hop artist filmed his YouTube Rachel Ehmke tribute video "Guilty" in the school hallway. Other musicians wrote songs to support teens who were being bullied. The over seventeen thousand views of a Rachel Ehmke video included some of the following comments:

"Just a few weeks ago our youth group pastor said we need to watch our words."

"Words hurt."

"This is a wake-up call."

"Why did you have to do this?"

"At first I thought this was a sick prank."

"Come on Kasson Mantorville, you are stronger than that."

"She left the whole town in tears."

"You never deserved this."

"RIP"

The last comment was "God Be with You."

Friends and students created an antibullying Facebook page.

Songs were written and put online to honor her memory.

All were ways for a community to mourn and express their sorrow. And yes, there were even a few cruel online comments about the memorials, including ones saying Rachel should have been stronger in facing the bullies.

Social media can make it easier to be mean, Mary said. It changes the dynamics of a relationship because you do not see each other face-to-face. "It's perhaps easier to hide behind the keyboard." Kids must be careful with how they use their words. "It's a coward's way. If you have something to say, say it to my face."

There are more difficult pressures for teenagers these days, Mary said. "Social media is not a good way for insecure middle schoolers to feel validated." And the constant media barrage can be overwhelming for that age group.

At the time of Rachel's death, a Minnesota task force was studying the issue of bullying and the state's thirty-seven-word antibullying law, considered one of the nation's weakest. Children wrote to lawmakers in a two-year legislative battle to enact a new antibullying law and testified before the legislature. Finally, an eleven-year-old boy joined Minnesota Governor Mark Dayton at the April 2014 antibullying law bill signing. He told the crowd how bullies at school had attacked him as a seven-year-old, laughed at him, and even threatened to kill him. "Today marks the beginning of a change in thinking about bullying," Jake Ross said. "I am very happy for this day." He'd had to transfer from his school, and he empathized with other bullied children. "I wish you freedom from your pain."

Mary established the Rachel Ehmke Endowment Fund with funds going to antibullying projects. An elementary school teacher who had enjoyed Rachel's second-grade class so much that she'd applied to be their third-grade teacher created a peace garden at the elementary school. Students can meander along its paths and read inspirational and antibullying messages.

Mary also has made a point of reaching out to parents who have lost a child. She wants to help them see that the intense, overwhelming pain of grief will subside; it does get better. To hear that from another parent who has lost a child to suicide can be life-affirming.

A parent whose son died in a traffic accident reached out to Mary shortly after Rachel's death. He provided impactful, timely help.

"Any parent who has lost a child becomes part of a club you never wanted to be part of," Mary said. It is hard to explain, but there is a heart-to-heart connection, an immediate understanding. "You just know."

"It's not supposed to happen that way," she said, with a child dying before the parent. And when it's self-inflicted, that's an even bigger kick in the gut.

Mary said it has taken several years of hard work and relying on her faith for Mary to speak publicly about her arduous journey since Rachel's death. She looked out her office window at a "Stop Bullying" purple-and-white banner, placed along the busy street years ago to raise awareness. And it needs to stay there, Mary said.

It is the people who are left behind who struggle. They are the suicide survivors: parents, best friends, siblings, and others.

Mary wants people to know that they can make it through with professional help, support, and faith focused on loving hard work.

The incredible support from Mary's close-knit family was crucial to her healing. Mary, Rick, and their extended family decided it was essential to take the annual trip north to the family cabin the summer after Rachel passed away. As difficult as it was, Rachel would have wanted that, Mary said. Rachel loved those summer vacations, filled with swimming, tubing, and sitting around the campfire at night.

Employees have provided additional strength to Mary, part of the fourth generation of the Tollefson family, to manage the business. And community support has been so important. Some people may avoid mentioning Rachel because it might make Mary sad. But Mary said it is helpful to continue the discussion about her. "You want to talk about good memories. You want to know that she is remembered, that she is not forgotten."

Taking positive action, like supporting antibullying work and groups like the National Alliance on Mental Illness (NAMI) and awarding scholarships to students so they can fulfill their dreams, have been other ways to move forward, Mary said.

She also used money set aside for Rachel's college education to give out Kindness Scholarships to Rachel's graduating classmates in 2017. Ten students received scholarships ranging from one thousand dollars to five thousand dollars. "It was one way I felt I could honor and remember Rachel—and also her classmates—as they suffered a great loss too," Mary said.

Family photos rim her office desk area, providing a backdrop of support. Rachel's bright smile in her seventh-grade school photo stands out. Mary turns and looks out her window. "I can still see her walking by the window, waving, smiling" as she stopped by the office after school to say hello.

Mary said that one of the hardest parts today is not knowing her daughter as an adult. What would be her dreams and her favorite things to do? Where would she go to college? Rachel had a lot of interests. They could have been enjoying outdoor adventures together. "But I am not complaining," she added quickly. "I love life. Every day truly is a blessing."

She feels closest to Rachel when she is in nature. Likewise, Mary feels a palatable comfort when she is out in the woods or by the pond.

"People say that time heals. I don't know about that. At times, perhaps. Sometimes it seems like yesterday. But you're never done grieving. You may heal, but it is always there." She may feel like she has made progress, and then suddenly, something will lay heavy on her heart, and she'll burst into tears. But after a lot of hard work and years later, it has gotten better. "And I don't feel the need to explain my tears."

There are still those times when things start to go on a downward spiral, centering on what she has lost. When that happens, she focuses on staying in gratitude and making her gratitude list. "Life is about being grateful.

"Rachel's death changed me. It made me a kinder, more empathetic person," Mary said, adding with a chuckle that she hoped she was kind before all of this happened. "I want to be there for others.

"No one ever said that life was going to be easy. But it's important to remember that while so many of us strive to appear that everything is good from the outside, we don't know what that person is facing. You know, the 'always be kind, for everyone is fighting a hard battle' idea.

"Who am I to judge?"

For years after Rachel's death, Mary had feverishly tried to find the answer to *Why?* She has replaced her question with *Why not me?* One of her favorite books, which she has read and reread, is Rabbi Kushner's *When Bad Things Happen to Good People*. It happens.

"I'm finally okay with not knowing the why. Now. Finally.

"I will know one day. I tell Rachel, 'I'll see you one day. I've got some life to live down here,'" to spend time with family, help others, and "do what we can do down here to make other people's lives easier."

Craig

One pleasant summer day in Clear Lake, I glimpsed the bright orange flag coming around the corner of City Park.

It was Craig Humburg on his bike. He was a familiar sight, riding around town on his recumbent bicycle, always ready to share a big smile and a wave. He stopped for a sip of water, so I parked my car and scurried over to him. I wanted to say hello and tell him how inspiring he was to so many people as he cheerfully made his bike tour around the lake and beyond each day. So many community residents were aware that Craig had been diagnosed with Lou Gehrig's disease, which causes eventual paralysis of muscles and nerves.

He shrugged at the notion of inspiring people. He loved bicycling. Then Craig explained the reason for his smile: he intentionally chose to focus on being grateful for an unexpected result of his illness. Because of Lou Gehrig's disease, he was at home and could help take care of his newborn first granddaughter. Had he still been in the workforce, he would not have had that time with her.

"Oh my ..." was all I could reply.

A quick smile, and he was on his way.

It's that attitude, those choices, the prayers, his loving marriage, his sense of humor, his grandchildren, his bike riding—that is what powers Craig Humburg these days.

As a former high school athlete and avid bicyclist and runner as an adult, he relies on Craig-powered mobility. Craig recalls that even as a kid, he loved feeling the sun and the wind and, most importantly, the freedom of bike riding and being under his own power. He was one of the early adopters of the sleek, drop-handlebar, ten-speed, derailleur-geared racing bicycles in the 1970s. Craig was part of the clusters of ten-speed bicyclists who raced around the lake before heading off to the countryside. While some friends later exchanged their bikes for car keys, he had developed that love of bike riding and never quit.

Craig encouraged his older sister Sally to try biking instead of always riding a horse in her free time. "You're not as limited as you are on a horse." Craig laughed. And before long, she was hooked on that sense of freedom too.

Throughout school, Craig enjoyed improving his athletic abilities and building physical endurance. Of course, one would never hear humble Craig talk about this, but he was on the Clear Lake High School's record-setting basketball team that had been the first to have an undefeated season in the conference. And it was just the second Clear Lake team in history to have earned a berth at the state basketball tournament. Ever since they were in seventh grade, the seniors on this team, including Craig, had worked to get to the state tournament. "We had a tremendous season," Coach Jim Ahrens said in the high school annual. "Our team was composed of a fine group of young men dedicated to accomplishing the goals they had set for themselves."

Craig applied that same discipline and rigor to be on the high school cross-country team.

The tall and sturdy man also applied this discipline to become a skilled carpenter who'd built a reputation for excellence. A local home-design consultant said he was part of a crew who were all amazing craftsmen. They could accurately and thoroughly assess a big project before starting, plan it, and then methodically proceed to enact their plan, each staying on task until its artful completion.

But in 2006, Craig noticed that his hands were starting to cramp up. Then he could no longer hold his hammer. His local doctor said he had some fasciculations—muscle twitching—in his shoulders and chest. The physician sent his patient and friend to a neurologist to confirm his suspicion.

The neurologist's diagnosis was awful to hear. "Who could ever expect something like that?" At age fifty-one, Craig was diagnosed with amyotrophic lateral sclerosis—ALS, more commonly known as Lou Gehrig's disease. Doctors told this professional carpenter that this terminal illness would cause progressive degeneration and eventual paralysis of his muscles and nerves.

"We weren't given a guarantee about life, that it was going to be easy," Craig said. "You do what you can with what you've got."

Doctors don't know why ALS occurs, according to the Mayo Clinic. Eventually, this motor neuron disease affects the control of the muscles needed to move, speak, eat, and breathe. There is no cure for ALS. More than five thousand people in the US are diagnosed with ALS yearly.

A colleague noted that Craig continued working as long as he could—longer than most people would. But then it became too difficult. So friends, church members, and community residents held a fundraiser for the Humburgs and built a handicapped-accessible addition to their house for when Craig would need to use a wheelchair. They were so grateful for that, Linda and Craig said, tears welling up for both of them. And yes, it was difficult for Craig not to be able to help with the construction.

They met with doctors, did extensive research, and joined ALS groups to gather information on how to face this diagnosis. The doctors said he shouldn't exercise. "But I'm kind of stubborn," he said, laughing. He knew he had to keep up his physical strength and mental attitude. And, of course, that involved biking.

Craig would pedal around the lake as soon as the weather warmed up enough for decent biking. With the orange traffic

15

safety flag fluttering over his recumbent bike, he would make his daily cruise. Sometimes grandchildren joyfully rode in his lap, and as they grew up, they cruised with their grandpa on their bikes while Linda pedaled alongside the whole crew.

Over the years since his diagnosis, he has clocked thousands of miles on his bike. "It is my freedom."

Taking the family dog for a walk also has been a vital release. They usually walk downtown toward the lake. Since Craig can't hold the leash, he wraps it around his waist. Their dog Ruger loves the walks, but he never pulls too hard. "He just knows," Linda said. She and Craig nodded in agreement.

Doctors gave him the sobering news of an average three-to-five-year life expectancy for ALS patients. But Craig has never been one to be complacent with average. Instead, he focuses on those who exceed average.

ALS organization staff have provided important resources and information on the disease through the years. Riluzole is one of the few medicines that has shown a temporary impact on the progression of ALS. Craig took this for a year and a half, but he saw little difference. The out-of-pocket cost for this drug can be about $1,200 per month for someone without insurance or third-party coverage. There are clinical trials on ALS, but research so far has provided nothing definitive on a cure. Support groups can be helpful for newly diagnosed people to learn about what to expect, but there currently is not one in Craig's area. There is useful information online, but "Don't believe everything you read on the internet," Craig says.

Craig, Linda, and the family suffered another tragic blow when Craig's beloved older sister died from a bicycle accident in November 2014. "It was horrible," Linda said. "Craig and Sally were very close." Sally and Craig shared their love of biking. Her obituary noted that the sixty-two-year-old frequently pedaled over ten thousand miles yearly.

Her son Seth also is an avid bicyclist. "After it happened, people would ask me if there was anything they could do for me," Seth told a local newspaper reporter. "The one thing I keep telling people is live—go do what you love because life is too short. A few seconds can change everything."

So how does Craig deal with so much?

"I pray a lot," he said. Craig has always had a strong faith. "Why else would we be here," unless there wasn't God, he asked. His faith has gotten stronger since he was diagnosed. "I was supposed to have been gone a long time ago." Instead, he focuses on thankfulness for what he has, like spending precious time with grandchildren, Linda, and family, instead of focusing on what he doesn't have.

As physical changes happen, Craig and Linda continue to adapt to live life to the fullest. They are using a tandem bike to continue riding those important bike rides. He joked about resorting to a motorized bicycle someday.

For several years, Linda has fed her husband using a feeding tube. This procedure became necessary when he could no longer swallow or lift his arms. In addition to ensuring proper hydration and nutrition, it reduces the chance of pneumonia. She helps him bathe and with other personal hygiene. "It's all the little things that we take for granted that are the hardest," he said. They've started using a machine at night that helps give his diaphragm a break by managing air flows.

Linda works as a receptionist in a medical clinic, but that doesn't mean she has any medical training, she said with a laugh. But she has been able to learn how to operate all the devices. "It can be a struggle, but we manage," she said.

The sense of sight, touch, hearing, taste, and smell are not affected since ALS attacks only motor neurons. But it has gotten harder for Craig to speak, a normal part of the disease. Linda sits directly in front of him, gently patting his leg, helping him express his comments, and then repeating them to ensure her interpretation was correct.

It is clear they can easily anticipate what the other will say. But, of course, part of that comes from having been married for thirty-six years. They are so grateful for that. And being married that long seems to be more of a rarity these days, everyone agreed.

Oh sure, they get mad at each other occasionally, but it turns out Craig is "always right," and so that settles it, he said with a good-natured teasing glance at his wife. They met at a bike race in Clear Lake on Memorial weekend. He was a bit shy, but "it was love at first sight, as they say," Linda said. They got married just over two months later. And they didn't have to, Linda quickly added with a smile.

Linda has been caring for Craig by herself all these years. So how does she explain the choice to care for him at home? "Craig is …" Linda pauses, searching for the words, "he is such a good guy," she says, tenderly patting his legs as she looks at him, tears welling up. "I couldn't think about not caring for him."

A hospice nurse and support team recently started coming to their home to provide physical, emotional, mental, and spiritual assistance. Linda and Craig were grateful to learn that hospice offers palliative care services in the home and more traditional services at their facility.

Even though Craig is losing some muscle strength, he is still mobile. So sometimes, unfortunately, people stare when they are in public places. That is hard on any ALS patient and their family. "It doesn't define the person who you are," Linda said. "When I see that, I just think, *They should have seen you before all of this started happening.*

"This doesn't define him," Linda added.

The conversation shifted to the decorated Christmas tree in the corner.

It's a busy, high-energy household when all of their grandchildren are there, they both agree.

Craig and Linda said they love being grandparents.

Plus, you can give them all the snacks and let them do the things you didn't allow for your children, Craig said with a grin.

Surrounded by his family, sixty-six-year-old Craig Humburg passed away on September 20, 2021.

Hedi

Love Thy Neighbor
(No Exceptions)

That is where Hedi Weiler plants her flag.

As a child, Hedi, her mother, and her sister hastily abandoned their Hungarian home, narrowly escaping the oncoming Russian army in World War II. For more than a year, they wandered homeless across Europe, hungry and fearful of dying in a bombing raid.

After being smuggled across borders and fearing being taken to a slave camp, they moved to the United States, where they gratefully began a new chapter. Twice, Hedi survived a devastating cancer diagnosis.

Many people could become embittered by such experiences. But Hedi has resolutely ensured that her heart remains open instead of hardened. A superficial understanding of her life experiences would be that Hedi is a *survivor* of a world war, homelessness, and cancer. But anyone who knows Hedi realizes that she is a thriver, driven by a passion for serving others despite her personal circumstances.

Whether teaching others to share compassion and peacefulness in an embattled world or starting a blog at age eighty to share health research, this Renaissance woman does everything with the enthusiasm of a college co-ed.

Where do we start?

As Hedi would say, "Just begin. It will unfold."

Hedi grew up in the then-Hungarian city of Sombor, located close to the famous Danube River in southeastern Hungary. It is now Zombor, Serbia.

She fondly recalled playtime with her cousins—they swam in the Danube River, had tea parties with their dolls, and played games outside. Her favorite pastimes were when she and her sister Hildegard went to their grandparents' home in nearby Miletitsch. Some of her best memories were of climbing trees and riding their bikes or homemade scooters—after doing their chores. "We were spirited kids," she said with a grin.

She gazed at the family photos of everyone dressed in traditional countryside clothes with shawls, some with their long hair braided atop their heads, while others wore black babushkas. She showed a photo of her younger self in an elaborate dress she wore for her First Communion. Everything was handmade at that time, she noted. Her father, a former Olympic wrestler, had two butcher shops and an import and export business, Hedi explained, so they were solidly middle class financially at that time.

Sombor's rich history also included being at the center of centuries-old, deadly tugs-of-war between powerful empires and nations. Danger loomed again as Hitler's National Socialists party rose to power in 1933 on its nationalist and racist platform, and World War II ensued.

As warplanes flew overhead, "there was always a sense of danger and fear; you never would know what might happen," Hedi recalled. They had air raids while at school. She remembered the terror of heading home from school "to see if her mother was still alive." Adults warned children never to pick up a toy left in the street—the partisans might have attached a bomb to it.

Even in the war's waning days, as Hitler's troops lost ground on both fronts, Nazi leadership insisted they would prevail against the approaching Red Army. But many Germans in Eastern

Europe started to flee west in a last-minute and chaotic path. The two young sisters nervously watched the exodus of other townspeople packing whatever they could from their homes and leaving in wagons to get ahead of the invading Russians. Longtime friends would stop for a final hug. By this time, her parents had separated. But Hedi's mom said they would not leave "because they were citizens." Before she was married, Hedi's mother, aunt, and grandfather had worked in the United States and had gained citizenship. The United States and Russia were allies. They would be safe.

They then started hearing about atrocities the Russians were committing as they battled westward—nailing people's tongues to tables, ripping ears as they stole earrings, and assaulting girls and women. The local commandant told Hedi's mother that she risked her family's life by staying, and finally, her mom decided to join the last military convoy leaving town. They haphazardly stuffed clothes into suitcases. No toys. No dolls. Nine-year-old Hedi and seven-year-old Hildie could only take what they could carry. "We felt fortunate that we could get a ride and get out of danger," she said.

From 1944 through the war's end, they were refugees in Hungary, Czechoslovakia, Austria, and, finally, Germany in its last shell-shocked, war-torn stages. Children, women, and older men were crammed into cattle cars to escape the invading Russian army. Excruciating hunger and thirst tormented the young girls. "If you ever have been starving or thirsty for a period of time—intensify that by days," Hedi said. "We never knew where they were taking us. We were simply refugees." The smells in the cattle car were repugnant from diarrhea, vomit, and everything else. They felt it good fortune if they ended up near a vent in the railcar.

They were regularly on the move to the next city and then the next because of bombings by the Allied forces on German-held cities at this point in the war. Refugee trains also were being bombed, so the trains sometimes stopped inside a tunnel for protection. One time when the train halted in the darkness, panic ensued as a rumor started that other refugees had been gassed while waiting in the tunnel. They also feared the tunnel would collapse. Officials funneled refugees into whatever building had been selected as the next camp and later stood in long lines for whatever watered-down soup or food was rationed to them. If there was still electricity in the bombed-out buildings that served as camps, lights remained on to keep mice, rats, and bedbugs away. The girls' nighttime ritual was combing the lice out of their hair. Soap and clean water were nonexistent, so lice-created skin sores became painful lesions.

As the older sister, Hedi said she "always had to be strong. Even though there were times that I wanted to be the one to whine, 'I can't carry this any longer,' I had to be strong." They focused on survival. How did she endure it? "Keep your focus—get on the train. What do I need to do to keep Hildie safe? There was always the next thing I had to deal with."

Hedi shifted the conversation, preferring to focus on when people showed compassion. She recalled a scene that brought tears to her eyes. "We heard the train grinding slowly to a halt. We don't know where we are. We hear the doors being unlocked and then creaking as they are painstakingly pulled open. A chill pours into the car. Fresh air, fresh air! One by one, we make our way to the opening and see two men standing there, holding gunny sacks. The sacks were full of freshly picked apples, which they handed to each person crammed into the cattle cars." Biting into that apple was as vivid an experience to the eighty-five-year-old woman today as it had been to the nine-year-old girl. "How grateful we were," Hedi said. "Could one have asked for anything more at that moment? It was like manna from heaven."

To this day, apples have "a lot of emotionality around them," she conceded.

"It's a block of my life that is still there," Hedi said of the fearful memories of her wartime childhood. Seeing a war scene or hearing gunshots in a movie can reignite it. "Honestly, that is still there at times," she says. And that is when she reminds herself, repeating over and over, "You are safe, you are safe."

After the war ended, they wanted to return to their grandparents' house, but they could not because their town was included in the redrawn borders of what had become Yugoslavia, and the borders were closed. They stayed with her mother's friends in Hungary, but work was scarce, and Hedi's mom knew her children needed to be with their grandparents. Hedi's grandfather had been a procurement officer in the Austro-Hungarian Empire in World War I, so he understood how to work with occupation armies. A neighbor with property on both sides of the new border profited by smuggling people across the border. The two sisters were smuggled, one by one, into their grandparents' hometown of Miletitsch.

The girls kept a low profile, but eventually, local officials allowed them to attend school. One day, townspeople staged a community parade, and Hedi and a classmate had the honor of carrying a massive picture of the new Yugoslavian president, Tito. Hedi offhandedly commented that she would be glad when the day was over because the image was so heavy to carry. The local police commandant got very upset when he heard her comment. Their grandfather assured the official that Hedi had meant no disrespect, but he still took Hedi and Hildie to a farm far away from there for a few weeks to be safe.

The situation grew even more worrisome when all fourteen- to seventeen-year-old boys and girls, including two of Hedi's cousins, were told to meet in the town square the next day for a "work detail." Families feared they would not see their children again. However, the youth did return after ten days of working in a brick factory.

Hedi's mother, still working in Hungary, had also been working feverishly to take her family to the US. Finally, she received word in August 1946 that they could board a ship for

America if they could quickly make their way to France. Smuggling was the only way out. The neighbor usually took one child at a time, exchanging for another, unbeknownst to the border guards. But this was so urgent that both needed to leave simultaneously. The two sisters lay motionless under a blanket in the back of the horse-drawn wagon. Liquid refreshments distracted border guards while the girls shuddered with fear under the blanket.

Finally reunited with their mom, they made their way toward the American consulate in Paris. They hurriedly boarded the troop transport, the USS *Ernie Pyle*. But the war was not entirely behind them, as the sisters saw soldiers hoist black body bags of passengers who had died from wartime illnesses into the ocean.

"Coming to the USA was a tremendous joy to us," Hedi said of the indescribable feeling of entering the New York Harbor in September 1946. Finally, they could attend school again, be together as a family again, and perhaps have their own home someday. They began assimilating immediately, speaking only English at home to become fluent. A friend of the family took them in for a few months. "We felt pure delight when we were eventually able to have our own apartment," Hedi noted. They shared their new home with other relatives when they migrated to the US. After the experience of being homeless during the war, having "our place again filled us with tremendous gratitude. In all these years since then, we have never taken home for granted. It has always been of great importance to us."

Hedi's mother worked hard to provide for her family, doing factory piecework and later working in a printing company. Hedi and Hildie both had part-time jobs while going to school. "Even though there were struggles, the prevailing feeling of gratitude for our good fortune and for being in the USA never left us," Hedi said. "We were glad for the opportunity to work hard to create a good life."

Hedi said she admires her mother's ability to have shepherded her family safely throughout the war in Europe and to their new home in the United States. "She was the one whose strength, fire, and leadership got us and those traveling with us through those refugee times. It was primarily women, children, and older men since the younger ones were in the army. They all depended on her.

"When I think about it now, I am amazed to realize that she was only in her late twenties to early thirties during these years. She was truly a woman ahead of her time in so many ways."

Education was a high priority. Hedi was determined to erase the gaps in her schooling due to the war and have formal education beyond secondary school. "What you have in your head, they can't take away from you," Hedi said her mom and family emphasized.

She graduated as a registered nurse from the Grant Hospital School of Nursing in Chicago in 1956 and later earned her bachelor's degree from DePaul University in Chicago. She had lots of friends and enjoyed her work. Then along came a special man, Frank. Hedi pulled out a wedding album and shared some beautiful photos of the handsome couple and their wedding party at their large church wedding. They had such fun that day, she said with a smile. And, of course, they had a big dinner and danced after the ceremony. Hedi loves to dance.

Frank was a "genius and a big thinker" and had a corporate job in Chicago, Hedi said. But ironically, he ended up taking over the family dairy farm in Wisconsin, "even though he hated cows." So, they moved to the farm and looked forward to the day they could raise their family.

She planted a vast garden and learned to can vegetables. Hedi acknowledged part of the reason for this was because she still fixated on the fear of "when the Russians come." Their relatives or refugees might need shelter, so she needed to ensure they had plenty of food and supplies. "It was a full life" with the farm chores and working full-time as a hospital nursing supervisor. But they made the time to go on memorable trips with their nieces and nephews.

While they cherished each other, it became clear that they might not be able to have children. Adoption was not an option because Frank felt it was paramount to pass on his genes. Frank eventually asked for a divorce. "If only you weren't so perfect in every other way," Frank told Hedi.

Hedi didn't want things to be acrimonious. She didn't want people to feel sorry for her or angry with him. And besides, she assumed the problem was with her. They parted as friends.

She started work on her master's degree in mental health/psychiatric nursing at the University of Wisconsin in Madison. Faculty member and friend Pamela W. introduced her to the holistic body-emotion-mind-connection medical approach and UW Professor Dr. David Graham's specificity of attitude theory, which posited a connection between a person's attitude and their diagnosis with certain diseases. "It opened up a whole new door," she said. "It was just unbelievable."

A few years later, however, the thirty-nine-year-old suddenly started hemorrhaging. "It was like being hit with a cosmic two-by-four," Hedi said. She wondered if it was related to the divorce, which was still a great sorrow. She was diagnosed with uterine cancer. "I was at a decision point. I thought, *It could be a rather painless way to die—to bleed to death.* I went through preparation for the dying process.

"But then," Hedi said with characteristic determination, "I set that aside. I had decided, 'Let me get on with what I am supposed to do.'"

Doctors scheduled surgery and radiation treatments. Hedi was determined not to have side effects from the radiation, so she and Pam W. dove into researching everything connected to healing. Then she applied the new techniques to herself. "Since I believed my healing was successful with the aid of them all, there was no ambivalence on my part."

She experienced no radiation burns. And one day, she visualized an image that "all of the cells had curled up and disappeared." And the cancer was gone.

After her personal health experience, she began a lifetime journey of learning more about the connections between the mind, body, spirit, and physical health. She became a board-certified, advanced practitioner and studied with Dolores Krieger, a New York University School of Nursing professor who pioneered therapeutic touch in the United States. Therapeutic touch is a contemporary version of several ancient practices to stimulate the body's healing process and is now in widespread use in hospitals and health centers worldwide.

Hedi later was part of the founding staff at the first holistic health center in Madison, Wisconsin, and did pioneering work in complementary medicine using sound, color, visualization, and others. Unfortunately, severe hip dysplasia resulting from her cancer radiation deterred her from pursuing her doctorate. But ever learning, she extensively studied and later taught classes on psychosynthesis and started her own counseling practice. She also established the Center for Awakening, an online resource network.

My sister Sue always wanted to learn new ways to better herself and enjoyed Hedi's classes and retreats. I attended my first one after Sue's passing, probably as part of the grieving process and as a way to connect with my sister's friends.

Hedi's gratefulness for each participant provided a calming segue from a hectic world into one in which to peacefully explore how we each can be of greater service to one another and humankind. Hedi could help others see the good in difficult times. "One of the gifts of crisis is that something new can emerge," she said. "I do have a choice in how I deal with challenges."

Major colon surgery later sidelined Hedi, and she moved to Charlotte, North Carolina, to live with her sister Hildie. Feeling the world needed to understand the horrific impact of war on children, Hildie started writing a memoir about their childhood experiences as World War II refugees. She wrote about the flashbacks she suffered as an adult as she relived the fear, panic, and anxiety of those times. "I write these memories of this time of war as a legacy to future generations, so that some connections to the past will be known. It was a sad time in history; I pray that it will never be repeated. May this book bring hope to children in the twenty-first century."

Hildie was diagnosed with pancreatic cancer and died in 2009 before it was published. Hedi's friend and a college professor helped Hildie with her manuscript in those final months and, after Hildie's death, oversaw the final publication of *Blueness of a Clear Sky: Memoir of a Danube Swabian Refugee and Her Journey to Healing.*

Neither of the sisters had shared their childhood wartime experiences with their families, so the book helped open a window of understanding. For example, Hildie's son Kenneth wrote in the book's epilogue about how his then-elderly mother had panicked when the tornado sirens suddenly went off while visiting him and his family. "It took me a bit to understand what was happening," Kenneth wrote. "My mother was reliving the experience of being bombed, and the sirens were the soundtrack of a terrible part of her youth ...

"With the wisdom of middle age, I now see that my mother had a choice in life," Kenneth wrote. "The experiences she survived could have driven her to live a life of fear or anger or aggression or hopelessness or self-destruction. Instead, she chose love, peace, caring, and self-betterment. Her choice made all the difference in my life, and for that, I am eternally grateful."

"I feel blessed with all that life has brought me," Hedi wrote in *Blueness of a Clear Sky.* "This is not to minimize all that happened during the war, nor a number of other difficult life challenges. It's that I see a life full of purpose and meaning. Each experience provides an opportunity for learning and evolving. Life is a great mystery—an adventure in which I feel fully engaged."

In 2013, Hedi faced another life-threatening diagnosis of cancer. She had a sarcoma in the muscle along her spine.

Rather than despairing, Hedi used the Caring Bridge website to update friends and family and express her gratitude for their support. It also provided Hedi with a teaching opportunity to deal with life challenges.

Hedi needed surgery and radiation. "Usually, I feel calm and peaceful and put my attention on all there is to deal with, step by step on this journey," Hedi wrote on May 18, 2013, on Caring Bridge. "If I have a short time left, I'm prepared for that. If I wind up having more time, the Divine always seems to have something for me to do, and I'll gladly do that. In either case, I'm paying attention to all this opportunity has to offer and trust in whatever the eventual outcome is. My love to all of you. Hedi."

After her final treatment before surgery, Hedi said she felt calm by repeating the words:

"Beloved, I am in your hands, I am in YOUR care … Till then, balance, calm, trust, steadfastness, peace, harmony, calm, calm, calm, love. Love, Hedi."

The surgery went well, and about one year later, Hedi wrote that her MRI and CT scans were clear. She wrote: "Most significantly, I continue my regular attendance and participation in the life of my wonderful faith community, The Religious Society of Friends (Quakers). The experience of being a member brings me tremendous joy. There are so many levels of experience but being a part of an active, loving community is simply beautiful and fills my heart …

I'm blessed with dear family and friends and great support. So many of you have been traveling this journey with me. I can only say, it makes all the difference. Thank you, thank you, thank you. My love to all of you, Hedi"

"I'm good to go," Hedi wrote later. "It's a good thing, too, since my 'assignment' in this life seems to continue. There is truly no lack of opportunity to serve. That truly delights me.

"I am grateful that the Divine still has use for me. My mantra is that I'll do whatever you ask me to do, just give me what I need to do it. I don't want to leave this planet without being used up."

In October of that year, friends came from across the country to celebrate her eightieth birthday with a potluck, singing, music, and dancing. Hedi admitted she was up until 2:00 a.m. playing Rummikub with her niece and nephew. She later surprised herself by joining Facebook and starting an online blog after being coaxed by friends to share her life experiences and wisdom. "Not even in my wildest dreams (I've had quite a few) did I ever imagine that I would write a blog.

"Either this is my time to go Home, or I have something more to learn," she wrote as she blogged on a wide range of topics to live healthier, fuller lives, including Alzheimer's prevention, nutrition, quantum physics, and many others. "A well-stocked mind is safe from boredom," Hedi noted.

Hedi's final blog post, "Compassion Matters," was written at 3:00 a.m., after what she said were months of thinking about it. How does one respond to disasters, tragedies, public vitriol, or someone's personal crisis? "Dear Ones, let us join together and pour our light and love over the darkness. Let us be aware of the Great Love that holds us together always…"

Hedi Weiler passed away on December 21, 2021, at age eighty-five. Friends from around the world joined in a Zoom virtual meeting to celebrate her life and service to humankind.

Mary Ann

Compassionate. Mischievous. Visionary. Loving.

They were all components of the Mary Ann effect.

The first time he saw her was at a favorite local restaurant, a speaker recalled at her funeral service. He noticed that lots of people were coming over and hugging her. *She must be someone special*, he observed. As he got to know her, he learned that for himself.

He learned she was the type of person who had traveled the world but never made anyone feel less important because they had not. She was a hard worker on many volunteer boards that she believed served essential purposes. And she was always up for fun times like a game of cards or conversation about the latest best seller.

She was everyone's friend, adviser, confidante, cousin, and stand-in mom and grandma. Her serene and gracious presence, however, could belie the impish and, at times, risque' jokes. She had graduated from the Minneapolis School of Anesthesia, and I would dare say that a surgery room would be the *only* place where this lively woman would put someone to sleep.

It was hard to imagine that this kind soul had endured physical and verbal abuse from her husband, Tom. His brain tumor caused a Jekyll-and-Hyde transformation from a loving husband, father, and visionary businessman into a sarcastic and volatile dependent.

I first got to know Mary Ann when she had an in-home nursing service and helped care for my gram, who had congestive heart failure. She was the personification of nursing professionalism and was very proud of her nursing experiences in the surgery room, teaching, and creating her own in-home nursing service. She took her nursing so seriously that she made sure the Nurses Oath Pledge was included in her funeral service:

Nurses Oath Pledge

I solemnly pledge myself before God and in the presence of this assembly to pass my life in purity and to practice my profession faithfully.

I will abstain from whatever is deleterious or mischievous and will not take or knowingly administer any harmful drug.

I will do all in my power to maintain and elevate the standard of my profession and will hold in confidence all personal matters committed to my keeping and all family affairs coming to my knowledge in the practice of my calling.

With loyalty will I endeavor to cooperate with other workers and professionals on this work and devote myself to the welfare of those committed to my care! So help me God. Florence Nightingale Pledge, Farrand Training School for Nurses, Detroit, Michigan. 1893.

Attendees at her funeral service nodded in agreement as the pastor read this. But there were audible chuckles during the part about abstaining from whatever is mischievous. Many of us thought she had brushed over that part.

Her good-natured bantering helped her patients and clients relax, even when they knew they would still get an enema. Thanks to Mary Ann and her assistants, my gram could stay in her home until she passed on. That was such a blessing. After my grandfather suffered a major stroke, he was in a short-staffed nursing home where patients had to compete for care.

But while her daily care schedule never skipped a beat with my gram, Mary Ann's personal life was topsy-turvy. Mary Ann's husband, Tom, was a successful businessman who had worked for the Woolworth Company and Ben Franklin Corporation. Theirs was a busy life, with their two children and Tom being transferred to numerous locations as he climbed the corporate ladder. After settling in Clear Lake, he and a partner were successful shopping mall developers and had a leasing business in the boom years of shopping malls.

Subtle physical changes, however, started to become more noticeable. Tom was diagnosed with brain cancer that oncologists determined was terminal. Of course, Mary Ann felt it was her responsibility to care for him at home. And raise their children. And generate some family income. Physical changes in Tom morphed into personality changes. First, it was verbal abuse. He spewed invectives at Mary Ann's friend and their neighbor Eleanor, whose husband had been killed when they lived in New York City. At times, he tried to hit the love of his life. Some people feared him and didn't know what to say, so Mary Ann's family became isolated. A good family friend was the only one Tom allowed to help with his care. This friend helped shield Mary Ann and the kids from his abuse. She said Mary Ann tried to care for him at home for too long.

Finally, Mary Ann moved him to a residential care facility. But he wandered away, tried to get home, and was almost hit on a busy highway. So there was always something to worry about and not many to lean on, Mary Ann said. But my mom provided a shoulder, and Mary Ann would always and forever be grateful to her for that.

Thomas Flaten succumbed to the brain tumor at age forty-seven. Mary Ann made a book for the kids and grandkids to remember him as the loving father, husband, Sunday school teacher, and church board member he was.

She moved away to the Twin Cities after his passing but eventually returned to Clear Lake, moving just down the street from us, perhaps as fate would have it. At a couple of points that summer, I needed someone to give me shots, and Mary Ann was just the nurse to help.

Mary Ann decided it provided an excellent opportunity to tease one of our elderly neighbors who made watching over the neighborhood his full-time occupation. So at about seven o'clock every morning, Mary Ann donned her bathrobe and paraded down the street to our house. The curtains at the neighbor's house would slightly part each morning as our neighbor peeked at Mary Ann strolling down the sidewalk in her bathrobe. Her adventurous humor made the shots more palatable.

Mary Ann became a member of our extended family, and we asked her and our good friends to be godparents to our son. Mary Ann promptly pronounced that she was his fairy godmother and could still see the magic dust on him as he grew older.

Mary Ann loved celebrating birthdays, so a good friend Marsha, my mom, and I started a tradition of celebrating one another's birthdays with unique experiences. Perhaps one of the most memorable birthdays was the progressive birthday celebration. We started at a popular city park so our birthday girl, wearing her festive crown, could hand out cake to strangers passing by. The next stop was at the local, rule-bound public library. Mary Ann was a library employee at the time, I was on the library board, Mom was an avid library user and supporter, and my friend was a well-known businesswoman. I'm sure that our older-ish group of women looked innocent enough. But since we were about to violate several rules, I was on the lookout. Meanwhile, Mary Ann lit the bright pink naked-woman candle she purchased while on a trip in Seattle as we sipped wine and ate food, giggling like schoolgirls. It was classic Mary Ann.

As fun and socially freewheeling as Mary Ann was, she acknowledged some compulsive habits. Her hair was a significant one. Every Saturday morning, she had her hair done at precisely the same time. Layers upon layers of hairspray ensured it would never be out of place. I teased her that she should carry a squirt gun in case someone walked near her with a lighted cigarette. But despite that neatnik hair obsession, she so loved reading stories to children at the library that she was always willing to squash her hairdo into whatever funny costume went with that day's stories.

Then there was her obsession with Norwegian heritage and Ole-and-Lena jokes. Those are big in the upper Midwest, home to many Scandinavian immigrants. And many of the jokes have a rather ribald twist, making them even more fun. On the more serious side, Mary Ann honored her heritage by creating beautiful needlepoint pillows and wall hangings with a distinct Norse flavor.

Mary Ann loved to travel, whether to Scandinavia or other places worldwide. She loved to learn, and she loved history—traveling was a powerful way to do both.

She was the consummate hostess, and like so many things in her life, she anchored that generous hospitality in her strong Christian beliefs. One of the many scriptures she chose to include in her funeral service is the following: "Let mutual love continue. Do not neglect to show hospitality to strangers, for by doing that, some have entertained angels without knowing it" (Hebrews 13:1–2).

And, of course, she couldn't just settle for cooking exceptional food. She took particular delight in the flambé showy cooking technique, where she could douse brandy over hot food and ignite it. She got into such a routine that we started to share our concerns that she was a bit of a closet firebug. But, of course, that suspicion just motivated her to do more.

"Oma," as her grandchildren would call her, treasured her family times. Her Facebook was full of family photos of her children and grandchildren and Mary Ann impeccably dressed, hair perfectly coiffed, in a boat, in a restaurant, at a party, or at a family gathering in Minnesota.

She loved her extended family, which seemed to grow like a never-ending conga line at a party. One of her favorite stories to tell was how shocked her grandson was to see a photo of her godson, our son Chris, on her refrigerator. "Who is *that* kid?" he demanded to know.

Mary Ann was one of those best friends to so many, always there with a shoulder to lean on, ever willing to listen as though she had no troubles of her own. She made people feel valued, a friend tearfully said after her funeral. That friend observed that Mary Ann had to rebuild her sense of worth, her notion of family, and her friendships after her husband died. Mary Ann wanted others to understand that we each have the capacity and inner strength to rebuild and renew ourselves after heartbreak.

Mary Ann helped my family when we learned that Dad had Alzheimer's. She helped us when sister Sue was diagnosed with stage 4 breast cancer. She read our comments at Sue's funeral service in Clear Lake because we did not feel we would be able to read them ourselves. Mary Ann even finished a beautiful needlepoint pillow that Sue had been unable to complete. She gave that treasure to my mom.

But Mary Ann didn't just listen to people's needs; she also was a woman of action. When she saw a need, she took steps to fill it, joining the boards of the local library, school, church, county compensation, cancer society, and One Vision, the nonprofit organization that provided services for her husband, Tom. Mary Ann saw the need for guardians of terminally ill adults with no family to care for them, so she organized a local chapter. Mary Ann saw the need for a local HIV clinic during the AIDS crisis, so she spearheaded that. Mary Ann was not timid about voicing her comments on issues, but everyone could count on the ideas being well researched and well reasoned.

While she was proud that she could manage a house with a large yard, a business, and other activities, the time came when Mary Ann pared down her furniture and other treasured belongings and moved into an apartment downtown. Correction—Mary Ann and her toy poodle, Stella, moved into an apartment downtown. Unfortunately, the view from a second-floor apartment wasn't as great for Stella as it had been from her front window perch on the couch, but the activity downtown made up for it. Dogs typically were not welcomed into Main Street stores, but Stella became the exception as she attained celebrity status in this small community. The post-grooming pink ribbons and her "This is what SPOILED looks like" T-shirt probably helped open doors.

It was hard when Mary Ann's four-legged, constant companion passed on. "I am doing well, but I really miss Stella," Mary Ann emailed me. "She really filled this little apartment with her huge, darling personality."

Even as she dealt with her own serious health issues with cancer and a stroke and experiencing the deaths of more friends, her circle was always open to new friendships.

She wouldn't tell people when she needed help or even when she was going in for medical tests, much to the chagrin of those who wanted to help. But she never stopped saying thanks to me for getting her a walker with a basket she used to transport groceries or books from the library. She loved that it was bright red, ensuring that this "old lady" could demonstrate she was still full of pizzazz.

Her faith kept her grounded through all of life's ups and downs. She had a talent for comfortably including a Bible verse in her lively, everyday conversation about one of her personal experiences.

She lived out her deep and abiding faith with love and compassion toward others, whether in her career as a nurse, serving on numerous boards of organizations, or being a legal guardian for several individuals through the years. Her funeral service selection of Luke 15:3–6 about the parable of the lost sheep fit Mary Ann's lifetime creed of including everyone in her social circle.

Mary Ann was her usual cheerful self at our annual Fourth of July party. It was always a treat to have her there—everyone enjoyed talking with her and hearing about her latest adventures. Her son, his fiancée, her daughter, and her fiancé had come to Clear Lake earlier so they could spend time together. Her Facebook page was full of vibrant photos of family get-togethers from that week. Just eight days later, Mary Ann suddenly passed away from a massive stroke, thirty-two years to the day after her beloved Tom died.

Mary Ann's apartment building neighbor summed it up for everyone a few days after the shock of losing her. This soft-spoken man, who had some disabilities, regularly stopped by our office to chat or share that he was praying for someone in need. Visibly very sad, Tom C. said nothing but held up a piece of paper with the name Mary Ann scrawled on it. "Pray for our building," Tom said and turned and walked away.

Of course, Mary Ann had prepared her funeral service so her family would not have to worry about it. And true to form, it had plenty of levity alongside the serious topics. She had asked her granddaughter to read a story about one of her recent nursing school reunions. The story, much to her granddaughter's horror—but probably not to her surprise—included references to how her body parts just didn't look quite the same as when the nurses had been young co-eds …

One of the hymns Mary Ann chose for her funeral service says it all: "Take My Life, That I May Be" written by Frances Ridley Havergal in 1874: "Take my life, that I may be consecrated, Lord, to thee; take my moments and my days; let them flow in ceaseless praise."

On February 4, the birthday following her passing, friends and family shared on Facebook how much they missed her as they toasted her and wished her a happy first heavenly birthday.

A toast to Mary Ann, indeed, on a life well lived.

Sue

To Everything, There Is a Season

"I just love the spring!" Sue proclaimed, arms outstretched, reaching for the sky. "It makes me feel so alive!"

She gathered her bathrobe around her and walked past her April calendar and her cheerful "Why Do When You Can Overdo" sign in her kitchen. Outside, the warblers and goldfinches were gathered at her many bird feeders, pausing for respite during their annual migration. The frogs had already brought in the new day with their guttural songs, toning like Tibetan monks to praise the morning. She walked past the bird and prairie wildflower books lying open on the kitchen table and the bookshelves brimming with classics, novels, and stargazing books and headed back to her comfy living room chair to gaze out on the landscape toward the lake.

By mid-May, sister Sue would join the Great Migration.

Summer Storms

Like a summer thunderstorm in the Midwest, sometimes there is little warning.

To those paying attention, there may be a distant rumble of thunder. Then the wind will switch, the temperature will drop, and soon, a relentless curtain of rain appears, drenching all in its wake. You can panic and try to lash down the kayak and bring in the lawn chairs. Or you can wait it out, realizing there are things beyond our control.

Sue had left a phone message asking my husband, Tom, and me to call that night after we tucked our son into bed.

Distant thunder.

Both Sue and Kevin got on the phone. Something was very wrong.

The wind started to shift.

Sue cleared her voice. She said that a biopsy had revealed she had breast cancer.

The torrent was fast approaching.

My heart was pounding. "The surgeon thinks I should have a mastectomy right away," Sue said. "I would like everyone to please be with me at the hospital." Sue never asked others to do things for her. Of course, we would be there.

I dashed out into the storm to tie everything down. The waves were rolling over the dock, and it was getting slippery. Suddenly, a crack of lightning pierced the sky. I had to do something. A gust of wind hurled a life jacket off the boat and into the water. I reached down, and a whitecap snatched it away from my grasp. *Why, oh, why?*

I couldn't sleep. I couldn't stop looking for more information on breast cancer. How could this be? It only happens in TV shows. Sue had done all the health things she was supposed to do—had her checkups and mammograms. She was smart and well-read.

"Shouldn't you get a second opinion? Do you need the mastectomy?"

"I just want to be rid of this," my dear sister said.

How can this be happening?

Storms, crises, and tragedies are inevitable for us all.

So how do we make it through those times when we feel our hearts breaking?

We Can Show Up

Show up for your loved ones. Be there in mind and body. Be there, even knowing it will hurt, because who wants to see a loved one suffer? But know that it will make a difference. Showing up means being there throughout the inevitable roller coaster of life.

As a family, we didn't have a tradition of openly demonstrating our emotional support for one another. Oh, we would hug, kiss, and gather for important holidays and events. But if we were hurting, we would walk that path on our own, like a Native American elder walking away solo to her deathbed. My sisters and their families lived in different cities, so when Sue asked us all to be there for her breast cancer surgery, it was nothing short of a miracle that everyone was there. We all just showed up in that hospital room.

Sue said she would lead the prayer. We all bowed our heads and remained quiet. *She will be okay,* I thought. *She is my big sister.*

The nurse came to take her to surgery, and there was a jumble of hugs and kisses. Prayers. And waiting. And prayers and waiting and waiting some more. My mom had quit smoking, so cigarettes were no longer a solace. Out came the tiny chocolate bars and then a book for diversion.

After an eternity in the waiting room, the surgeon opened the door, glanced at everyone, and asked Kevin to step into the hallway. The surgeon felt things went well, Kevin later told all of us. She had removed Sue's entire left breast and felt confident that it was an early-stage tumor. Chances for a long life multiply if there is early detection.

We all breathed a collective sigh of relief.

The Waiting Rooms

Our next goal was to get Sue home and comfortable and keep her free of infection and lymphedema. She was a great patient.

She had done lots of research and followed the American Cancer Society's Reach for Recovery aftercare instructions.

We all tried to focus on her care rather than worrying about the upcoming pathology report.

Five long days later, Sue received the results. The pathology report showed that the tumor was twice as large as initially estimated. In addition, cancer was in eight of eleven lymph nodes tested. That meant cancer had advanced elsewhere in her body.

Shock and disbelief.

We were told that her cancer stage would be determined by how far the tumor had permeated. However, that would require more tests. And Sue needed to heal from the surgery before tests could be done.

Sue didn't talk about how it had felt to lose her breast. Instead, she focused on recovery and suggested we all do that too. It was painful and exhausting to recover from the surgery, but Sue didn't complain. She had always been physically strong. Sue amazed us as teenagers when she waterskied around the entire lake while the rest of us dropped after a few crisscrosses over the boat wake. She hopped on her bike after school and took thirty-mile trips before supper.

Sue would be okay. She had always been tough.

I tried to corral my mind if it started to slip into what-if questions. I focused on learning more about breast cancer since we had no family history. Reliable, user-friendly information was not widespread on the internet; there was no Google then. It took going to the library and bookstores and talking with medical professionals.

Sue already had some resources because she felt it was important to know about her health. We worried Mom could get lung cancer from smoking, but our family had no cancer history. As I learned more about breast cancer, lots of questions surfaced. Why hadn't a biopsy been done after Sue repeatedly expressed concerns? Why hadn't other tests been done before a significant disfiguring surgery like a mastectomy? I had lots of questions.

I wanted to support my sister and thank the surgeon, so I tagged along to her follow-up appointment. I thought it was odd the surgeon didn't make eye contact with me even though I introduced myself and said thanks when we shook hands. She quickly looked at Sue's incision and wrapped up the brief meeting with the assurance that Sue was stage 2 at most. We both thanked her for her care.

I headed back home. Time was passing. We tried to go about our daily lives while waiting until Sue had healed enough to have further tests to determine the stage. The stage, 0–4, reflects how far cancer has spread and helps the oncologist assess treatment. There are charts and diagrams to correlate the stage and prognosis, but I avoided them. My sister didn't fit any charts.

More time passed. Sue went in for the tests. More waiting.

And then the phone call. It was Sue and Kevin, not just Sue.

I could sense fast-moving black clouds starting to gather, like a Midwestern storm front suddenly appearing out of nowhere. "It's stage four," Sue said quietly.

It was like a swirling, churning mass of black clouds suddenly dropping out of the sky and onto the ground. This spiraling twister randomly leveled houses, downed power lines, and ripped trees out by their roots. Our lives were changed forever.

I wanted to reach through the phone and cradle my sister in my arms. "Susie, what can I do?" No one could say anything. "I'll see you soon. I love you."

Like a pendulum on a grandfather clock, my emotions swung from agony to sorrow, to disbelief to anger, and back and forth. How could this be happening to my sister? *I should have known somehow. What could I have done differently? I told her to see a different doctor; I should have taken her there myself. But I'm just the little sister; what do I know?* But first, I needed to reassure my parents, who lived down the street, that Sue would be okay. And I needed to tell our young son his aunt Sue would be okay. Plus, I needed to call my other sister, Sarah, and talk about supporting our sister and parents and assure them it would be okay.

Later that night, after my husband and son were in bed, I headed back to the computer and women's health books to check out my fears. I learned that the most critical question regarding breast cancer is whether it has spread to other organs. That determines who lives or who dies of breast cancer. Stage 4 is a metastatic tumor, meaning it has spread to other organs. And there was no cure.

I bowed my head and wept and wept. *God help us.*

Stuff Happens—There Isn't a Why

Why does our loving God allow suffering? And why did it happen to *my* sister?

> I don't know why one person gets sick and another does not, but I can only assume that some natural laws which we don't understand are at work. I cannot believe that God "sends" illness to a specific person for a specific reason. I don't believe in a God who has a weekly quota of malignant tumors to distribute and consults His computer to find out who deserves one most or who could handle it best. "What did I do to deserve this?" is an understandable outcry from a sick and suffering person, but it is really the wrong question. Being sick or being healthy is not a matter of what God decides that we deserve. The better question is "If this has happened to me, what do I do now, and who is there to help me do it?" (Rabbi Harold S. Kushner, *When Bad Things Happen to Good People,* Schocken Books, 1981)

> When times are good, be happy; but when times
> are bad, consider God has made the one as well
> as the other. (Ecclesiastes 7:14 NIV)

Sue had "done everything as she was supposed to do," Sue wrote in a later summary to give to her caregivers. But many disturbing things arose as she wrestled with the diagnosis and started to recuperate from surgery. When Sue was in her thirties, doctors weren't routinely recommending mammograms for her age group. But she had read that women should have a mammogram at about age thirty-five, especially if they had any risk factors. Sue had three risk factors: never being pregnant, having lumpy breasts, and being overweight. So Sue took the initiative to have a mammogram, which showed a hazy area in her left breast. They told her to come back in six months, and she did. Still nothing definitive.

Sue and her husband moved to another city, and Sue asked her doctor's office staff to send her baseline mammograms to the new physician. She had a mammogram in their new city to ensure that radiologists compared them. The next mammogram was still not definitive, even though Sue again mentioned increased breast pain. Meanwhile, she changed insurance carriers so she and her husband would have the same insurance. Her primary care doctor went on maternity leave, and Sue was assigned a different primary care provider. Sue noticed changes during her monthly breast exams and told the new doctor that her left breast was swollen, red, itchy, and painful. The doctor's response? Sue was overweight, and that might be causing the problem. Sue pointed again to the area she was referencing. The doctor replied, "What have you been doing to yourself?"

We three sisters were raised to be polite—at all costs. And to be respectful of authority. Sue was embarrassed and humiliated that the doctor had chastised her for doing something to herself as if to create a medical problem. Sue started questioning herself and her instincts. "Because she didn't seem to think that there was anything wrong other than that I was fat, I did not want to follow up with her," Sue wrote in a later summary. She again mentioned the inverted nipple and the continuing left breast pain with the new physician. She assumed they had read her medical history, had her baseline mammograms, and knew this was a recurring concern. The doctor said that was just a typical manifestation of her age and was not a concern. The doctor told Sue her fibrocystic breast condition could cause pain and lumpiness, but breast cancer doesn't hurt.

She was starting to feel like a hypochondriac. Cut down on caffeine. Focus on losing weight. Over and over.

Sue requested an ultrasound, noting that an earlier caregiver had told her that her breasts were too dense to get an accurate mammogram. But she was told no because those were only for women under age thirty-five. She also asked about having a needle aspiration, but doctors didn't think that was necessary since she didn't have a family history of breast cancer. In addition, doctors did not communicate that mammograms did not find about one in five breast cancers at that time.

Finally, a gynecologist became concerned enough about the appearance of her left breast that she asked a surgeon to do an exam. "I was really frightened at both appointments," Sue later wrote. But the surgeon said she didn't think it was cancer. "I was relieved," she said. "Since she had seen many breasts, and I had only seen my own, I trusted her judgment." Nevertheless, she said Sue could have a biopsy if that would make her feel better. Sue asked if the surgeon were in Sue's situation, would she have one? The surgeon said she wouldn't. And so Sue didn't.

Later, Sue had another annual mammogram, and oncologists detected a suspicious area this time. The same surgeon who'd said two years earlier that she wouldn't recommend a biopsy told her it appeared Sue had breast cancer. A biopsy confirmed it. She would lose her whole breast.

"So much for all those years of mammograms and exams!" Sue wrote later in her research summary. "Evidently, I was part of the 10–15% false negatives. Guess it was just my tough luck that they never bothered to try any other tests despite my asking. I was angry!"

Sue laboriously tracked down and pored over her medical records. She discovered that her previous physician's medical staff did not transfer her baseline mammograms and early reports to her current physician. She then learned that medical records were not shared between the different metro area clinics she had used for several years. In addition, record requests she had made to the other offices throughout the years had been fruitless. As a patient, Sue had assumed doctors were making recommendations based on her complete medical history. "No one seems to know where they are. No one knows how it could have happened."

All of this occurred at a time when there weren't standards for breast cancer diagnosis, health records were still on paper and not digitized, there was limited health information on the internet, and there was no centralized database of the latest research. It also was in the early days of HMOs; it was not unusual for the HMO to require patients to try less costly tests first to keep costs down.

And then we learned about the gag clause, a provision in some HMOs that prevents doctors from discussing all treatment options. The American Medical Association, consumer groups, and professionals allege that these provisions inhibited full and honest dialogue between doctors and patients that would have assured informed decision-making.

Lastly, we learned the heartbreaking information that the doctors and surgeons were part-owners in my sister's HMO. They may have wanted her to undergo a clinical trial so the HMO wouldn't have to pay for the treatment. The bottom line had been more important than my sister's health.

What do you do with that feeling of helplessness, of rage toward the system?

Never, Never Give Up

Sue was tired and felt trapped. She had done everything she was supposed to do. She had lost faith in the system. At this stage in the game, she needed to forget that HMO, said a good friend who had a lifetime career as a nurse. "She needs to hear outrage from other professionals. She needs to hear 'They were terrible to you.'

"Sue is fighting for her life. She needs all the support she can get. She can't battle this alone."

"Get out of that system! You deserve the best health care," I repeated on the phone, in faxes, and in emails. I researched well-known cancer treatment centers, most on different coasts or parts of the country. But Sue didn't want to be so far from her home, husband, and pets at that time.

"Cancer, more than almost any other disease, can be overwhelmingly complicated to treat," wrote *New York Times* reporter Denise Grady in a July 29, 2007, article titled "Cancer Patients, Lost in a Maze of Uneven Care":

> Patients are often stunned to learn that they will need not just one doctor, but at least three: a surgeon and specialists in radiation and chemotherapy. Diagnosis and treatment require a seemingly endless stream of appointments. Doctors do not always agree, and patients may find that at the worst time in their lives, when they are ill, frightened, and most vulnerable, they also have to seek second opinions on biopsies and therapy, fight with insurers and sort out complex treatment options.
>
> The decisions can be agonizing, in part because the quality of care varies among doctors and hospitals, and it is difficult for even the most educated patients to be sure they are receiving the

best treatment. Patients are told they must be their own advocates, but few know where to begin.

"You need to listen with a sorrowful heart," a friend told me. "And then help her see the opportunities to advocate for herself, for her to realize that *I am worth it*."

My best friend from college always provided thoughtful wisdom when I needed it. So I called her, mainly just to talk. It turned out that her sister knew a renowned oncologist in Atlanta. She called him to ask for recommendations. He responded that his friend and highly respected colleague was the director of a cancer center in the city where Sue lived. He offered to set up an appointment.

We emailed and faxed questions to ask him about hormone therapy, chemotherapy, clinical trials, pain, resources, the care management team, and complementary therapies. Finally, Sue got an appointment with the busy director of a significant multimillion-dollar cancer center. This man, who had achieved a nationwide reputation, took the time to listen to my sister's story, care, and provide options. And hope.

The director also told Sue that his wife had recently been diagnosed with breast cancer.

Her faith was restored at least enough to make an appointment with a new caregiver.

Sue emailed on November 23 about meeting with the new oncologist and explaining why they recommended tamoxifen therapy rather than chemotherapy:

> Even though it is in my bones, it isn't making holes in them now, which is good, and means that I don't have to worry about fractures. People live with this. That's the main thing …
>
> The main thing with Thanksgiving is to give thanks and have some fun, eh? I could use it, & I bet everybody else could, too.

I really feel pretty good. The surgery is healing up well and I can do what needs to be done. Things look way better today than they did Friday. I really think that I have a strong constitution and am pretty tough. Getting that old tumor out was important, now the tamoxifen and my body can work together to handle those nasty cells. Could have been much worse.

Love you a bunch,
Sue

Perspective

Tragedies can rip relationships to shreds or solder them together for eternity.

"It puts everything in perspective," said a good friend who was mourning the recent death of her young nephew. He was a full-of-life, athletic young man who loved the outdoors. Cancer caused paralysis and life in a wheelchair before it consumed him. "It makes you stop and think about what is really important in life," she said.

I began asking myself daily, "Is this a life-or-death situation?" As life's inevitable challenges surfaced, I would consider Sue's situation and my challenge. It helped me determine which issues were worth the time and energy.

Thankfully, Sue's lifelong zeal for learning, her constant desire for self-improvement, and her empathy for others ensured she would not follow the path of a victim. As a result, the diagnosis did not catapult her into a pit of self-pity. Instead, she decided it could provide combustion to ignite her essence.

And it provided necessary combustion for her family. It was tempting for all of us to take the path of denial or distractions so we wouldn't have to go through this frightening passageway. Wouldn't it just be easier to avoid, like the galloping circus horse that suddenly rears back and goes around the fiery hoops instead of through them? In some ways, perhaps. But a good friend liked to remind me that there is no dress rehearsal in real life. Life is short. Each day is precious. We are called to love and care for one another.

Sue decided that her cancer diagnosis had put a machete in her hand, empowering her to chop down the jungle of contemporary society, so full of distracting materialism, self-absorption, and disconnection, so she could instead reach a place of purpose.

Thankfully, Sue decided she would not be a victim. She chose to focus on living, not dying. *Carpe diem* prevailed when Sue's energy supply cooperated. She helped restore prairies in the Madison area. She attended conferences to network with people about the woods our family protected with a conservation easement. She kept biking and walking outside as long as her body allowed it.

Susan Kay Connell-Magee chose to focus on living, not dying.

Someday Becomes Today

Sue had often talked enthusiastically about how fun it would be to stargaze together. I remember thinking, *That sounds great, but I don't have time now. I've got this to get done and that to get done. But someday …*

A breast cancer diagnosis helps set priorities.

Let's stargaze.

I've always appreciated the awe of a starry sky. I liked to marvel that, despite our scientific explorations, we can't grasp space's magnitude. And I would pretty much leave it at that.

But not Sue. As an adult, Sue decided she needed to know more about astronomy. That meant she would learn the physics and chemistry of celestial objects, how ancient civilizations understood the night sky, and, well, you get the picture. It was classic Sue to tackle it all.

Major meteor showers were especially intriguing. We planned to watch the Leonid annual meteor shower in November. In the Midwest, the best way to view this miracle is while lying on the ground, swaddled in a warm sleeping bag. We went out at about 11:30 p.m. "Keep scanning the horizon because it will take time for your eyes to adjust," Sue said. "They aren't really falling stars," Sue added, explaining the science behind the marvel. Suddenly, "Whoa! There's one!" We scanned the horizon for more. "Wow! Did you see that one?

"The really, *really* big Ed-Sullivan-style show starts later," she said. She gathered up her sleeping bag and headed back to our parents' house, where she was staying. When the alarm went off at 2:00 a.m., I stifled a yawn and questioned my sanity. I glanced outside the bathroom window just in case there might be some action to see. Suddenly, a fiery red ball blazed across the horizon, seemingly leaving a jet stream behind it.

I'm in! Like a firefighter responding to a clanging fire bell, I quickly slipped on my clothes and tried to rouse a sleeping husband and, next, our son. No luck; their slumber was too sweet. Instead, I met Sue on the lakeside.

Sue unrolled her sleeping bag. But soon we realized the lights coming from the downtown area were too bright. Light pollution even in this little town. We sighed. We headed across the street to the garden, hoping not to wake the neighborhood dogs. "What if the neighbors hear us and call the police?" We giggled like kids. "Here, let's position ourselves so this tree blocks that streetlight ... Wow! There goes one! Did you see that?" I shrieked. "Whoops ... I'll try to hold it down."

"There's another!" we took turns exclaiming. "And another!" They were like fireworks blazing across the sky. But, no, they were much grander and more glorious than fireworks. I thanked

God and my lucky stars for allowing me to share this with my sister Sue.

In the darkness, I heard a muffled noise. "Are you okay?" I asked. I realized she was vomiting. "I just feel sick sometimes," Sue replied. "It's no big deal."

I made my wish on the next falling star.

Lean On

I deeply treasured the stargazing and other adventures, bittersweet as they were. But then big, hefty black question marks would appear and start to descend on my think-positive-thoughts process. And then it felt like my fears could crush me.

What if one of the clinical trials hurt her more than helped her? Was she at the best medical center and under the proper care? How could my son go through life without his aunt Sue? She was the one who had brought him so many books and the little reading chair with miniature armrest covers she'd made from the adorable Lone Tree Point Nature Area jacket he had outgrown. She was the one who'd bought him toddler books with Spanish words because she knew how important it was to learn Spanish at an early age. Who would teach him about the night sky? How could I stand not having more outdoor adventures with Sue, like camping at Glacier National Park, cross-country skiing in Yellowstone, or visiting Hopi and Navajo reservations together? Will our Sue turn into an emaciated older woman, like a family friend our age who had breast cancer? How would our family function if Susie wasn't with us?

"Listen to your sister with a sorrowful heart," a friend told me. But first, we must accept our powerlessness.

I tried to memorize St. Francis of Assisi's Prayer for Peace. I couldn't concentrate enough to learn it. Instead, I found a prayer card and carried it with me, leaving it on the bedside table each night.

"I want you girls always to remember the power of prayer," my gram told me years ago when I stood at her bedside. She hadn't felt well that day but didn't want to go to the doctor. She didn't want me to stay with her that night. But she repeated her comment about the power of prayer. Looking back, I know now that had been the beginning of her congestive heart failure. Looking back, I think she was concerned she might pass on that night.

I was determined not to be angry at God for what happened with Sue. Stuff happens. There aren't always answers. But Sue had shown such an example of gratitude that I wanted to ensure that our son would see examples of thankfulness for the precious gift of life each day. "So, let's start each day with this," I said to our son as he got in the car, and we headed off to elementary school. "This is the day the Lord has made; let us rejoice in it and be glad. Hooray!" And later, we added, "I dedicate my thoughts and actions and the fruits of my thoughts and actions to the Lord. Amen."

Every day we said that. No matter what Sue's news was, we said that.

And we said prayers, lots of prayers.

Gratitude and Thanksgiving

We humans can have an insatiable appetite for more, no matter how much we have received.

It's not a new concept. Even after being freed from slavery in Egypt, the Israelites grumbled about not having enough food or not having the right kind of food. And there is the classic story of a man at the circus, sitting front and center with a hot dog and popcorn in hand, gazing at the three rings of entertainment in front of him with the elephants, acrobats, rings of fire, and silly clowns. But he complains, "Where are my peanuts? Where *is* the guy with my peanuts?"

I thought back to our family's first Thanksgiving together after Sue's diagnosis. Sue had always loved Thanksgiving because of its focus on pure and simple thankfulness for life's gifts. She sent me a note telling me she just wanted to focus on being thankful for being together and not dwell on the cancer news.

It had been just a few weeks since her stage 4 diagnosis, and it was the first time we got to see her in person as we all met at the halfway point city. Mom was the first in line for hugs. We all tried to give them space. Next, "A big hug for Aunt Sue and Uncle Kev!" I said enthusiastically to our son, Christopher. Then it was my turn. I began to cry even though I had said I would not. Sue didn't look different. *Please let this all be a bad dream,* I thought.

"Please don't expect me to do all the possible treatments," Sue told me after the others headed to the restaurant. She had watched friends battle breast cancer. "I may not choose to go through all of them. They just may be too much." Her husband, Kevin, sadly nodded his head. I was stunned. She was a fighter, so I had assumed she would check out all treatment options. But I let it go. I just wanted to be near her. And Sue wanted us to focus on thankfulness.

It was Sue who led the prayer at the dinner table. We joined hands and said thanks for so many blessings, being together, having food to eat and homes to live in, one another, and the gift each day of life.

We followed the prayer with silence to somehow let it all sink in.

Then we searched for what we could talk about in this new normal of different priorities, a world that seemed out of control, and an unknown future. Talking about favorite teams playing in the holiday football games didn't pass muster. So instead, we were happy to focus on our son and our nephew's latest adventures.

We struggled to define this new normal and maintain the thankful spirit throughout the holidays. Our definition of good news was a moving target. Here is Sue's fax just before the new year:

Tuesday December 29, 1998

Hi Back, Jansie!

Kevin & I really enjoyed our holiday with you! Thank you for the warm hospitality! Got some good news yesterday: no brain tumors, according to the CT scan. Yay! We're looking forward to Erik's birthday, too. See you then & there!

Love, Sue

I bought "In Everything, Give Thanks" signs to place around the house as reminders to keep a thankfulness focus in the upcoming year. I jotted down many scriptures about remaining thankful amid difficult times. It's not being grateful *for* the circumstances but being thankful *in* all circumstances because we know that God is in charge. I read about Martin Rinckart, a shining example of thankfulness under challenging times. As one of the last surviving ministers in the walled city of Eilenberg, Germany, during the Thirty Years' War, he performed nearly fifty funerals daily because of war, famine, and disease. Yet he was able to write the classic hymn "Now Thank We All Our God."

While I researched gratefulness, Sue showed gratitude to her caregivers and others around her. She brought candy to the nurses who did her IV for the pamidronate to strengthen her bones. Sue wanted us to tell funny stories during her infusion sessions to lighten the sadness of others in the unit. She provided a meal to all the oncology clinic and cancer center staff members with the following note: "THANK YOU all for giving me and many other patients another year of high-quality LIFE! Your care, expertise, and kindness make a huge difference to me and many others. Here's to You! Bon appetite!"

Before discussing her terminal illness, she always asked her caregivers about their families. She even remembered family members and recent events.

Even with limited energy, she sat at her kitchen table, meticulously designing special calligraphy thank-yous and adorning them with watercolor flowers. In addition, she provided meals for her veterinarians because of the extraordinary care they had given to their pets.

While Sue showed gratitude because she knew it was the right thing to do, it also may have provided positive health benefits. Recent scientific research shows gratitude can help all of us. For example, grateful people have fewer aches and pains and better mental health and self-esteem; they are more empathetic and even can sleep better and longer. In addition, a 2003 study found that gratitude significantly contributed to emotional resilience following the 9/11 terror attacks.

As Sue's physical world shrunk around her as cancer progressed, her gratitude did not. Instead, she said thanks for the smell of food, even though she didn't have an appetite to eat it. As she became more bedridden, she talked about how much she appreciated an electric lift on the bed. If the bedroom windows were open, she could still hear the distinctive song of the sandhill cranes.

A Nation's Storm

While our small family was desperately searching for options for Sue's stage 4 cancer, a horrific storm was about to appear on a brilliantly sunny, bright blue sky day. The entire nation and world would soon witness the unimaginable scene of a jetliner filled with passengers crashing into the World Trade Center in New York City.

Everyone gathered around their TVs to see smoke pouring from one of the 110-story World Trade Center towers. Such a terrible accident, onlookers commented, until a second jetliner crashed into the other tower. Camera crews captured the pandemonium on the streets as Trade Center workers frantically escaped the buildings. Others jumped to their deaths as the massive towers began to buckle and collapse. Then, more shock and disbelief when news reporters announced that another jetliner crashed into the Pentagon. Yet another crashed into a field in Pennsylvania.

The United States was under attack.

The world watched in horrified disbelief. Bloodied survivors, coated in plaster dust, stumbled through the streets of Manhattan. Flames, smoke, emergency vehicles, and personnel filled the TV screens.

The newspaper headlines read "Terror strikes" and "Horror— Bush vows retaliation. Today, our nation saw evil." Ensuing days focused on stories of families searching for loved ones, tacking up posters, placing ads in newspapers, and calling names in desperation near the rubble in hopes of finding some clue of loved ones' whereabouts.

There were stories of immense pain, final phone calls with loved ones, and reports of miracles, courage, and heroism. All seemed underpinned by an unspoken recognition of the sacredness, mystery, and brevity of this physical life we all share.

We mourned as a nation and with others across the globe. We took extra care to tell our children and spouses "I love you" before heading off to school or work and after bedtime kisses. Across the country, people were flocking to churches and synagogues to unite in prayer. Billy Graham, the preacher who had counseled presidents for generations, spoke to a stunned and sorrowful nation from the National Cathedral on September 14, 2001.

"We come together today to affirm our conviction that God cares for us, whatever our ethnic, religious, or political background may be," Graham said. "The Bible says that He is 'the God of all comfort, who comforts us in our troubles …' We've seen so much that brings tears to our eyes and makes us all feel a sense of anger. But God can be trusted, even when life seems at its darkest.

"We are reminded of the mystery and the reality of evil. I have been asked hundreds of times why God allows tragedy and suffering. I have to confess that I do not know the answer. I have to accept, by faith, that God is sovereign, and that He is a God of love and mercy and compassion in the midst of suffering." The second lesson Graham told was one about "our need for each other … None of us will forget the pictures of our courageous firefighters and police or the hundreds of people standing patiently in line to donate blood."

And the third lesson was one of hope, of a spiritual renewal out of destruction.

Dad

My grandfather used to say, "When you have your health, you have everything." He lived a long, robust life until he suddenly was incapacitated by a stroke. My mom found this hardworking, energetic eighty-two-year-old collapsed in the bathroom, never to walk on his own again.

My parents had been pretty fortunate in the health department through the years. But we started noticing some changes with my father when he was in his seventies and still had not retired. I assumed the changes were part of the normal aging process. My primary focus was on our young son, Sue, and full-time work. True, he forgot where he put his keys, which was odd. But my workaholic father was still going to the office and seemed to be accomplishing things.

Then he developed a surprising interest in nationally advertised sweepstakes contests. Cheap prizes started showing up with regularity at my parents' house.

Sue was concerned that he was developing dementia, or worse, Alzheimer's. Unfortunately, there is no way to confirm Alzheimer's other than an autopsy at the time of death. But there were significant characteristics to look for, doctors said. They just weren't sure how to mitigate it. And they were confident that there wasn't a cure.

One late January morning, we all received a call from my sister Sarah's husband, Dennis, saying she was in the hospital for sepsis. She was ill, dangerously ill. My parents and I soon headed to the hospital as Sue also drove there. For the first time in our lives, I was the driver, and Dad was a passenger in the back seat. He kept telling me we were heading in the wrong direction. As we headed north on the interstate highway, a gentle snowfall soon turned into a whiteout. We regrettably headed back home again and kept in contact by phone. Sarah stabilized within a few hours, so we hit the road again the next day. We found Sue by Sarah's side at the hospital. "She had a dangerously high temperature," my brother-in-law said. "She almost died," he added quietly. We gave our prayers of eternal thanks.

My mom and I headed back there later that week to help Sarah after she was released from the hospital. My dad wanted to stay in Clear Lake.

Upon returning home, I discovered that the police had called my husband over the weekend. My dignified father, who was always immaculately dressed and known as the "silver fox" because of his full head of striking white hair, had gone to Clear Lake's famous Surf Ballroom over the weekend, wearing his pajamas and a coat. He didn't understand why they asked him to leave. After all, he and some other Clear Lake business leaders had owned the Surf for several years, ensuring that no one would demolish this historic icon during those lean years when ballrooms were out of vogue.

Weeks later, we found out he had been regularly going to a nearby restaurant and leaving without paying. The new owners thankfully recalled us all going in there together. They assumed we would be back to pay the bills.

His behaviors got more peculiar, not just in baby steps but in giant strides, like a slab of ice calving from the iceberg with a loud crack and the subsequent reverberation throughout the ice field.

His interest in the sweepstakes became an obsession. He stood by the front door, waiting for the mailman to arrive each morning. My attorney husband eventually sent letters to the sweepstakes companies, threatening to contact the state attorney general's office if they didn't stop preying on him.

Like a toddler in an adult body, he bounded across busy streets without even looking. He forgot to turn off the coffee pot. Due to the sunset effect, he could get angry with my mom, especially at the end of the day. Medications seemed to amplify the confusion rather than diffuse it. He sleepwalked at night and once unlocked the door and got into the street. We had to childproof the house. He went to the office, and I kept an eye on him to give Mom a break.

Thankfully, his golfing buddies invited him out to play a round. But eventually, even his favorite game in the world became too hard to play.

Mom and I went to a caregiver's support group. We tried to read anything we could about the disease. Unfortunately, there is no known cure for this relentless memory thief. Afflicted individuals lose more of their memory and abilities as the nerve cells are attacked and destroyed in the brain's outer layer. The time from onset to a total disability may vary from three to twenty years.

For my mom's sake and my dad's protection, we eventually and sadly concluded that Dad needed to be in a care center's Alzheimer's unit. The man who had survived the battlegrounds of Korea, was an army paratrooper instructor, and had served with the occupation forces in Germany after World War II now needed to be placed in a locked unit.

For months, we would regularly visit him at the care center. Other hollow figures walked the halls. We tried to imagine what their lives had been like before Alzheimer's. My dad would hug his grandson instinctively. He looked puzzled about the rest of our names. Then, when it came time to leave, we had to divert his attention so we could slip away and lock the door behind us. Our hearts ached.

On a Sunday night in late April, we had just returned from our son's out-of-town weekend soccer tournament when the phone rang. My mom said the care center had just called her to say Dad had been taken by ambulance to the hospital. He might not make it through the night.

Mom and I hastily drove to the hospital. We knew Dad had a cold, but how had it become life-threatening? It had quickly developed into pneumonia—the "old person's friend," as my grandparents softly called it in discussion with other friends. He looked terrible lying in that hospital bed. He barely responded to our voices, pats, or hugs. But we thought at some level he knew we were there. Mom and I camped out in the hospital room that night, occasionally dozing with one eye open and anxious hearts. Finally, morning came, and my dad had made it through the night. My sisters could come the next day and say goodbyes to their father. Sarah took a turn staying in the room that next night.

Hospice staff stopped by and explained their services. We weren't ready to throw in the towel, we told them. They noted that some people returned to their care centers or homes after being in hospice. They could provide palliative care so that he wouldn't be in pain. And it would be so much more peaceful than a busy hospital.

We ultimately agreed that it would be more peaceful, and the ambulance crew moved him into a hospice room overlooking a beautiful garden. "His comfort is our utmost priority," the nurse said kindly. Dad hadn't said anything since Sunday. He had a fish-out-of-water look that the hospice materials mentioned.

Friends came to visit. It was hard for them to see him like that. The only movement I saw from Dad was a decisive twitch as though he wanted to respond when a dear friend patted his hand and said tenderly, "May you rest in peace."

As evening came, the nurses made sure he was comfortable. They didn't feel his passing was imminent, so my husband, Tom, took my weary mom home. Again, I checked to see that Dad was comfortable and started to settle in for what I thought would be through the night into the next day.

I realized other family members had said their goodbyes to Dad, but I had not. Dad and I had butted heads over some issues when I was a teenager. But that is just part of growing up. Dad was a workaholic, so he was often gone. But of course, he wanted to provide for his family, and I thanked him for that again. All that mattered right now was his comfort and for him to know he wasn't alone. But then I felt this urgent need to verbalize my thanks for so much more. I thanked him for ice-skating and playing basketball with me. And for chasing after our dog Teddy Bear when he ran away with our winter stocking caps. And for putting up the basketball hoop in the warehouse so I could practice at night. And for letting me win at PIG sometimes. And for the Peewee, our little green wooden boat that we loved rowing in circles for countless hours on the lake. And for taking us waterskiing, snow skiing, and on all those picnics. So many things. I thanked him for being a good dad.

After giving Dad a kiss and a hug, I sat in the chair next to Dad and said a silent prayer asking for God's continuing comfort for my dad. Then, within what seemed like minutes, I heard a noise like a loud exhale of breath. "Dad, Dad, are you okay?" He was no longer breathing. The nurses had said his passing was not imminent, so how could this be? But he seemed to be leaving. *I love you, Daddy. I love you.*

Dad had broken free from the prison of Alzheimer's.

Forgiveness

Several people told us that Sue's healing might not be physical healing. Yeah, yeah, I did not want to hear that.

But that might have been the blessing amid such pain.

Time and experiences can separate us from our dreams and the innocence of youth. But hardships are an inevitable part of the human experience. And if we aren't careful, we can pile up our perceived injustices, including some inflicted on us by those closest to us. We can choose to see the pile or keep sidestepping around it as if it's a heap of dirty laundry on the floor.

Sue needed discussion to understand things, repair hurts, and forgive. Mom, however, had always avoided discussion like the plague. While we were growing up, we would come home from school and want to talk about the day with our mom. But she usually handed us a cookie to help us feel better, then announced it was time to run outside and play! Later, it was time to do homework in our separate rooms.

Anger and hurt were to be denied, not acknowledged. "Wait until your father comes home," Mom yelled at us after being spanked and told to go to our rooms. As a kid, waiting for that further punishment had been frightening and lonely.

When we had our son, I knew I had to break the cycle. We would not spank him as a method of teaching. The only exception would be a life-and-death situation, such as if he'd crossed a busy road. We were able to keep that pact.

Aunt Sue agreed on that course of action for her first nephew, also remembering the fear and loneliness of those times. Whether it was because of those experiences or despite them, Sue had always been ahead of her time, following the beat of her own drum. She was the first to walk down the sidewalk on stilts, ride a unicycle, get a ten-speed bike, and have cross-country skis. In addition, she got her pilot's license, something my dad, the World War II paratrooper, had always wanted to accomplish.

After high school graduation, she and a friend decided to get a Eurail Pass to have unlimited train travel in Europe. *Wow. How cool would that be?* I daydreamed. But I also saw my grandmother's tears when we shared a prayer for Sue's safe return. And then there was the late-night phone call the next year—Sue called our mom to say she had decided to leave college and had driven her jeep to Montana. She got a job with a geological survey company. As the youngest child, I was still living at home. I held my breath. "We'll go out there," my parents said—end of discussion.

Fast-forward to family dynamics when we were all adults:

I received a brochure for a forgiveness workshop and asked Sue to join me. Unfortunately, she was too exhausted from cancer to attend. But that reminded Sue of a vital goal she had not accomplished yet. Sue announced one morning that she wanted to talk with Mom about the suffering they'd caused each other throughout their lives.

Yikes! Not conflict, not now. I wanted to run away. I always tried to avoid conflict. But Sue and Mom sat at the kitchen table, and Mom listened, quietly and without avoidance, while Sue told her about some of the pains she'd had growing up, about how maybe they were too much alike, which was part of the issue.

But that was in the past. And this is now. Sue told Mom that it is vital for us to acknowledge that life includes pain. That can help lead us to forgiveness, which is essential. With that, Sue told Mom that she forgave her. She next asked for Mom's forgiveness and told Mom she loved her. Mom reciprocated the same statements, and they hugged for several minutes.

A few days later, Sue thought of a friend she also needed to forgive. Maybe she shouldn't have been mad for many years with a high school friend who'd missed her wedding. Soon, Sue and her friend had a meaningful phone conversation.

Sue and Kevin had significant discussions about what they could have done differently, but also of thankfulness for each other and Kevin's care since her diagnosis.

We three sisters talked about siblings' inevitable squabbles and how we wished there hadn't been any. We all agreed none of the hurts had been intentional; it was part of growing up. *Forgive us, Sue, for not always being aware of the times you suffered.* We talked about the great times when we all lived in Oregon. We agreed we wanted many more of those times together as adult sisters.

Sue asked me to forgive her for the possibility that she wouldn't be able to be my big sister in tough times forever. "I always thought I would be your protector," Sue told me. As kids, we were partners in crime, hiding under blankets with flashlights to read books long after we were supposed to be asleep. We sent each other notes attached to a string with a clothespin between our bedroom windows. "Here comes another one!" we giddily whispered as we heard the unknowing laughter of adults socializing downstairs.

Sue said she'd always felt she should protect me. How would she do that now?

Journeys/Fall

The Tamoxifen was starting to run its course. The reality of what could happen with stage 4 cancer was again before us. We did more research and had more questions for the oncologist. We needed other options. There must always be other options.

Sue was able to get into a clinical trial in Chicago that seemed to hold some real promise. She appreciated that it was in Chicago, a city she enjoyed and could drive to alone. The clinical trial would conclude just before Thanksgiving, and we all planned to gather again.

When we met at Sarah, Dennis, and Erik's house for Thanksgiving, Sue looked pretty in a holiday outfit, wearing a new dark brown wig that contrasted with her blue eyes. But something had happened. An incredible sadness hung over her.

After eating and gathering dishes, Sue finally revealed that she had been in a car accident while leaving Chicago. It was at the tollgate, she said with obvious disgust and disbelief. While leaning over to reach for change, Sue ran into a concrete divider. She was okay, but the car had to be towed to a repair shop. Sue was a great driver and traveler. Something had changed.

Our Susie began to cry—the first time she cried in front of all of us since her diagnosis.

Sue and Kevin came to Clear Lake that fall. We stargazed at night and had dinners at Mom's house. We went up on Walnut Hill at Lone Tree Woods, looked over what was then cornfields, and talked about the prairie restoration project. She was so excited that our family was moving ahead on it. It was as if she could already see the big bluestem and black-eyed Susans dotting the countryside. "That will be so good for the lake water quality, the wildlife, and the people," she marveled. And to infuse people's appreciation of this ecosystem by building a bike trail through it—she was so pleased.

Too soon, they had to head back to their home. After they left, I picked up some items by the lake and happened to look skyward. A cloud caught my eye—it was in the shape of a bird! It was an eagle or perhaps a hawk. I called my husband, Tom, to look at it. He agreed that, yes, it looked like the shape of a bird.

I didn't know it then, but that was to be Sue's last visit to Clear Lake.

Winter

Whiteouts.

In the throes of a Midwestern blizzard, it's easy to understand why pioneers sometimes tied a rope between their home and barn so they could feel their way back and forth. The ground, the lake, and the sky become a blur of frenzied churning. It is still a frightening, life-threatening experience for anyone to be trapped in a whiteout. Despite all our technology, highway traffic comes to a standstill. It takes time to get your bearings.

Getting a cancer diagnosis is like being in a whiteout. Everything comes to a standstill. It takes time to get your bearings.

The winds always do calm down, and the snowfall subsides. And if we pay attention, we may see new beauty left after the snowstorm, like Jack Frost's artistry glistening in the sunlight on our windows. We may notice a heaven-sent, giant sun dog prism of light suddenly hanging in the sky. If we listen carefully, we may hear the mysterious gurgles and pings of the frozen lake as it expands and contracts.

Similarly, after the shocking onslaught of Sue's diagnosis, we could choose to pay more attention to one another and enjoy the preciousness of spending time together. We all looked forward to gathering in one of our mutual favorite places at the restored Winneshiek Hotel in Decorah, Iowa, for Sue's forty-ninth birthday on January 3. This turn-of-the-century hotel has hosted notables from the king of Norway to presidents. The guest rooms feature antiques and plush creature comforts like down comforters and oversized, fluffy towels. Being there was like being a guest at Sue's house.

The three sisters and our mom had often gathered in Decorah for canoe trips along the Upper Iowa River with its limestone bluffs. Vesterheim, an internationally renowned Norwegian museum, was always a highlight, and this time, Sue pointed out some of the antique bowls she had donated to them. We celebrated Erik's upcoming birthday. It was a busy day, and our Sue was very tired. We gathered around her bed to sing "Happy Birthday."

The following month, Sue was excited to report that they got a hospital bed. The hum of the fax machine at 9:30 p.m. was a comforting reminder we were thinking about each other. "We kind of jerry-rigged it for tonight, but it is *very* comfy. Hope you had a good day. I'm looking forward to seeing you and Mom next week."

Kevin gave Sue a dozen beautiful roses for Valentine's Day. Their sweet smell permeated the kitchen. Sue meticulously changed the water and removed dead petals so the delicate flowers would last longer.

Sue had talked enthusiastically for years about a nearby prairie restoration conference. We agreed it would be great to attend since our family's prairie restoration project was moving ahead. For several years, Sue had burned prairies, restored prairies, and gathered seeds at local sites. I had so much to learn.

Sue took her typical copious notes and gathered more information for our family prairie project. I was so grateful to be there with her. Unfortunately, I found out later from Kevin that Sue had fallen and hit her head earlier that day. She hadn't mentioned it to me.

We had also looked forward to going to Canoecopia, a fun canoe, kayak, and outdoor expo. But Sue was too tired. "Please go and enjoy it for me," she urged.

Doctors determined why our strong Sue was getting weary— cancer had spread to her liver. Her oncologists were concerned and suggested the extreme measure of radiating it.

There were significant risks with this—how could this be the best approach? We tried to get other opinions. Maybe her oncologists were being too aggressive. Perhaps they weren't bold enough. How were we to know? They were the experts. I accompanied Sue and Kevin to some of her radiation treatments. "You guys are my pack," Sue, the dog lover, exclaimed as we all climbed in the car.

In between the treatments, there were lots of talks. "I can choose to accept all that has happened and go from here, live in the present, and enjoy my day," she said in one of her conversations with her mom and sisters. "I can't correct the past."

Springtime

"I just love the spring!" Sue exclaimed, doing almost a gentle pirouette in her kitchen. "It just makes me feel so alive!"

Sister Sarah and I took Sue and Kevin to eat at one of their favorite restaurants. As the hostess showed us to our table, I noticed several diners stared at Sue, then glanced away. I guess she didn't look physically well to others. I wanted to tell them she was much more alive than many in the restaurant. But I didn't.

Within moments of sitting down, Sarah asked Sue to tell us what she had learned since the diagnosis. My internal reaction was, *Stop! We're just having a pleasant outing so Sue can relax and be out of the house. We're not here to have profound discussions.* I was trying to signal Sarah across the table to cool it.

But Sue didn't mind. Instead, she thought quietly and responded, "I would have loved more, forgiven more, and been closer to my family."

Each of us sat silently, trying to absorb what Sue had just told us. It was such a profoundly sad statement about what could have been and, at the same time, such a profoundly wise statement about what can be. But unfortunately, we could not turn the clock back to do things differently. So, we could choose to despair about Sue's message. Or, we could heed this lifetime wake-up call to tell our family and friends that we love them and find ways to forgive one another. It is hard, so hard. Life is so short.

In our clumsy, fumbling way, we tried to listen more, love more, and be aware of what was happening at that time rather than worrying about future what-ifs.

When she had the energy, there were short but profound talks. Thankfully, Mom jotted some of them in her ever-handy, tiny spiral notebooks. Sue intentionally chose not to be bitter or angry. "We always have a choice of how we act and react," she said. "Everyone gets the whole package. I was given a second chance at life. I have learned a lot" and am a "better patient and a better person." She was armed with the knowledge that she could advocate for herself.

"I feel more powerful than ever before."

Sue wanted to ensure that we understood how much she loved each of us. She especially wanted Mom to know how much Sue appreciated her many loveable qualities, so she started compiling a long list of Mom's qualities.

I jotted down notes on things I wanted to tell Sue: ... *you're scared and so am I ... your gratefulness is so amazing ... do you know how much I treasure you ... be of a strong heart.*

We showed her numerous scrapbooks that Mom had compiled. We had fun discussing her ecology club and the recycling projects, student council projects, photos of complicated Halloween costumes she'd designed, and a boutique shop she'd opened as a high school sophomore.

One of her accomplishments was winning the American Bar Association Award in 1972. "The Bar Association Citizenship Citation is traditionally presented to those of the graduating class who have, by their deeds, most clearly indicated their resolute dedication to the principle that ours shall be a government of laws and not of men ... Law is essentially the resolution of human conflict. In that resolution, there are aspects of the human character which require uncommon tribute other than an individual's inexhaustible voice or his unyielding will, aspects such as compassion, tolerance, patience, perseverance, and a certain grace in the worst of circumstances. It is these characteristics, certainly, which the Bar Association contemplated at the inception of this award."

A certain grace in the worst of circumstances.

A Prayer for My Sister

I woke up with a start one morning while staying at Sue's house. I headed into the shower to appreciate the peacefulness of shower time, of uninterrupted thought to start the day, and it was one of those times when an idea needed to manifest itself.

As Sue's family, we still had the opportunity to tell her how much we loved her, help her understand the positive impact she had made on the world around her and the unique and special qualities that made her one of a kind. We could tell her that resounding message, but we could amplify it in the literal black and white of the written word. So I borrowed one of Sue's laptops and started writing. And writing. It came tumbling out.

I suggested that others start writing down their thoughts for Sue. Mom began, and then my sister Soz, Sue's husband, Kevin, husband Tom, son Christopher, and nephew Erik. Christopher wrote about everything his aunt had done as a high school student to help the community. He wrote about their nature hikes and how easily she could explain geology. "She has so much knowledge that if she wrote a book about everything she knows, she would never be able to finish it because she always learns something new every day about something or another. One of my favorite things about Aunt Sue is that she is always willing to cuddle or to have a hug. I love Aunt Sue so much that words cannot even begin to describe it."

One example of how much Sue's illness impacted our son was when the Sunday school kids were learning about Joseph and the coat of many colors his father had given him. The kids listed their personal goals on an outline of their Dream Coat. In addition to getting his black belt, becoming an NHL superstar goalie, and a few other wishes, this ten-year-old listed "Cure for Breast Cancer."

Rarely one to be on the receiving end, Sue promptly wrote her lists for others, starting with the top things "I LOVE about you, Mom," printed carefully and thoughtfully.

Despite its inadequacy, I was anxious for Sue to read what I'd written. But she was grateful and finally able to accept compliments.

Later that day, she reluctantly noted that there were a few dates that weren't quite right in what I'd written. We started talking about how fun it would be if she edited my work since she was such an excellent writer and editor. Much joy emerged from putting these thoughts down on paper. We called it "A Prayer for My Sister."

Like a lotus flower opening to a new day, these forgiveness discussions and A Prayer for My Sister opened doors to many other significant conversations, conversations where we all finally listened and absorbed. "I can't correct the past," Sue said. "I can choose not to be bitter or angry. I can choose to accept all that has happened and go from here. I can live in the present and enjoy my day.

"Today is a good day to be alive."

A Prayer for our Susan

Our Susan's world is huge and small. It's the Milky Way galaxy, and it's the dainty lady slipper flower in the woodland or bottle gentian on the prairie. It includes concern about whether the largest mammals on earth can complete their annual whale migrations back to the warm waters of Mexico or whether the tiny warbler will safely journey back to its summering grounds on the tundra inside the Arctic Circle …

The Long and Winding Road

We were all anxious about Sue's next appointment with her oncologist to see if the radiation had helped. I wanted to hear what she thought of the other oncologist's recommendation.

"Whoa! I haven't done my patient update," Sue remembered, and she shuffled to her computer. I was concerned it might wear her out before the appointment, so I offered to type it. She paused while the PC whirred on and then sat bolt upright in her bathrobe. Then, with steely determination, she started typing away at the computer. She knew what she wanted to accomplish.

I stepped back and settled into a comfy chair to wait for my strong-willed sister to write her patient update. Her newfound energy seemed to radiate from her, filling that part of the room. For these moments, my emaciated sister was in the driver's seat. She felt empowered to tell the doctors exactly how she had been feeling. Finally, she had found her voice.

I sat back and watched in awe. I found out later that despite Sue's increased pain level, Sue stated in her patient update that she was still interested in treatment if it offered a reasonable prospect of improvement or greater comfort. And she was still researching clinical trials and wondered if any might be an option.

We passed the "Today Is a Good Day to Be Alive" card Sue had posted in the hallway by the front door.

"I'm with my pack," Sue said as we drove to the hospital. When we walked through the hospital corridors, Sue pointed out that the cancer section had been redecorated. "They're always trying to freshen it up," she noted. We headed toward the women's bathrooms.

"I keep hearing 'The Long and Winding Road' playing over in my head," Sue said from her stall. We exchanged glances while washing our hands and headed to the waiting room.

The mood was somber as we headed into the exam room. Sue handed her patient update to her oncologist. The oncologist glanced through the two-page summary and laid it on the counter. "It appears that the cancer has spread," she said. "I'm afraid there is nothing more we can do for you. It would be best if you went home."

Or something like that. I am not sure. A voice in me was screaming, *Nooooooooooo!* I wanted to jump up and exclaim it. But instead, I asked if there were other options. The oncologist looked at me sternly and said in an agitated whisper, "That would be like spitting in the wind."

I hoped that Sue had not heard her comment.

We gathered up our things. Sue went around to the staff in the cancer center and thanked each of them for their care.

We headed home.

"I guess sometimes it's just a roll of the dice," she said softly in the car.

We entered the front door of the quiet and still house and walked past the "Today Is a Good Day to Be Alive" sign. There were hugs and tears in the living room. We were in a surreal time of uncertainty about what to do next.

"Do something that makes the day seem normal." Sue started looking at her mail. "I just can't talk about it anymore right now."

I picked up the morning newspaper. The headline was about President George W. Bush warning Saddam Hussein to leave Iraq within forty-eight hours because of his alleged weapons of mass destruction. *"All of the decades of deceit and cruelty have now reached an end," President George W. Bush announced on March 17, 2003.*

Try to do something normal. I put the paper down.

Everyone headed to bed early that night. Sue had been sleeping in her hospital bed alone because of the bone cancer pain. When I checked on her that night, Sue and Kevin were sound asleep, their arms wrapped around each other.

Acts of Desperation

Though the oncologist had said there weren't other options, I had to think there must be. Sue had to beat this thing.

While it's possible to discuss life-and-death issues at an intellectual level, there is an ongoing undertone of an inner primeval drumbeat, an innate desire to survive and for our family members to remain with us. I recalled how my grandfather's will to survive resounded even after a significant stroke had suddenly immobilized him. He had been a man of boundless energy who couldn't imagine confinement in his home, much less to his bed.

Sure, I tried to verbalize that I accepted the oncologist's message. But I was still actively looking for what was now becoming a miracle option. I followed up on off-the-beaten-path possibilities—something I would never have considered earlier. But at this point, I listened intently to anyone's hearsay stories of other cancer patients' actions. Some were still alive. I got details about local families who took loved ones to other countries for treatment.

And then I recalled the very helpful oncologist at the other clinic who had moved to a clinic in a different state. He returned my call the next day and kindly talked about how he remembered Sue. His comment on alternative treatment centers was succinct. "That would be an act of desperation to go to _____," he said. "It would rob her of the few peaceful moments she has." But he did call Sue to discuss some possibilities of clinical trials and palliative treatments to help her feel better.

In March of that year, I wrote this letter to Sue:

Dear Susie,

"I want you girls always to remember the power of prayer."

Our Gram told us that, for all of us to remember, forever. I didn't realize it at the time, but in retrospect, I think Gram thought she was dying. There she was upstairs in her bedroom, lying on her bed. She wouldn't let me stay with her that night. She said she was OK and that she didn't need any help. But it was clear that she felt very strongly that she wanted to communicate a vital message, a life-saving message, a message of strength and comfort.

It's one that I've wanted to tell you, Sue, for a long time. Prayer will give us the strength to handle whatever comes our way. God is there to help, always, within us, to surround and comfort us, to lead us to people who can help us during our time on earth. God can help heal us in all the ways we need to heal. It's just a matter of asking for help. Somehow, none of us can do it alone. I have so much to learn about letting go and letting God take over. For the past several months, I keep hearing "Thy will be done" from the Lord's Prayer. After hearing that all my life, it is starting to make some real, personal sense. And I have been reading and rereading St. Francis of Assisi's prayer, "Let me be an instrument of thy peace … let me sow love where there is hatred …" it was like the clouds parted and the sun shone through. We are here for each other, to help each other, to let God's love shine through us …

It has been so difficult since you were diagnosed with breast cancer. There is no denying that. It has been heartbreaking. Lots of tears have been shed. In so many ways, it still seems unreal … But through it all, the strongest emotion has been the love that I've felt for you. I want to be able to protect you and insulate you from this and any hardship. But, yes, I know it's not within my power to do so. So, I have to let go and turn it over to God.

Love you, Jan

The trumpet-like, yellow daffodils were resplendent that Easter. Our families usually celebrated Easter together, typically going to church, eating together, then having an egg hunt. Sue wanted to be together, and we gathered at Sue and Kevin's home. Getting dressed up took most of her energy. She agreed to let Kevin bring a wheelchair to the restaurant. She was exhausted after a few bites of the Easter meal. But we were united in the celebration of Easter, of new life and new hope.

Sue wanted her nephews to enjoy their egg hunt, so we hid the treasures around their front yard. Sue watched from her wheelchair. She had the sunken cheekbones of an elderly woman; her shoulder bones pierced the back of her blouse. But her joy of watching her nephews cavort around the yard held her upright.

Surrender and the Power of Prayer

Back home, I regularly got down on my knees in our living room and prayed to God for a miracle. I read and reread the scripture sections about miracles. I knew I needed to learn much more from the Bible, and have I prayed enough? Even though I gladly prayed for others, it was hard for anyone in my family to reach out and ask others to pray for us. We didn't want to impose on others when they had enough of their own problems.

Plus, there are so many people in such pain. I prayed for the 9/11 victims and their families. With such tragedy for so many, I worried that praying for our small family might seem selfish to God. After all, we could still hug each other. We could still tell each other the words we meant to say. And then I remembered Gram's bedside exhortation always to recall the power of prayer. Miracles were happening in New York City. God is all-powerful. Maybe it was okay to pray for Sue too.

I prayed that I would not feel angry about my sister's medical treatment—or the lack of it. Greed was a reason they'd sidestepped the proper treatments. Greed drives tobacco companies to make addictive products despite knowing they will cause horrible lung cancer deaths and contribute to breast cancer and other health issues. My parents had to grapple with the possibility that their smoking had contributed to Sue's breast cancer.

But why does Susie need to suffer? Why such pain? How about a miracle? The planet could sorely use a miracle these days, Lord.

Thy will be done. When bad things happen, you mold the shattered pieces into something whole again. But what? And when?

I'm trying to surrender. I'm trying. Please, please, help us.

Portals

I hadn't put my suitcase away for months.

By leaving it half-cocked against our bedroom wall, it was a portal, a connection to Susie—even though I wasn't with her, I was there in my heart. It was a sign that I could quickly hit the road for Sue's house if necessary. It was a reminder that we are all travelers, all of the time, each on our own journeys.

I left our annual Clear Lake Earth Days events early that spring. Sue insisted that I participate because we both were actively involved in Earth Days. I finished tossing things in my suitcase and hit the road. I was so fearful and full of so many questions. I feared I might hinder more than help this time, or perhaps I'd say the wrong thing. I feared something might happen to Sue while I was there or that something had happened. I felt guilt and sadness about leaving my boys—husband, son, and pets included. I passed through Minnesota into the gently rolling Baraboo Hills that Sue loved and toward Madison's lakes.

Sue and Kev were in the front yard when I got there. Sue's emaciated body was leaning to one side of her wheelchair, like the pose of the older adults you try not to wake in a nursing home. Kevin met me at the driveway. "Sue just hasn't been able to communicate much the past day or so," he said softly. "Thanks for being here."

I hugged Sue and tried telling her about Earth Days because she'd always loved to hear about it. "Hmmm ... good," she murmured with a slight smile and then went back to dozing in the warm spring sunlight. We sat quietly together. We heard the ancient *karoo* of the sandhill cranes as they headed for their wetland bedrooms for the evening.

"Should we head inside, Susie?" I asked.

"Not yet," Sue replied. "Not yet."

It was the black vomit that sent me reeling early the following day. Our Susie was getting worn down, one punch after another, like an already dazed and bleeding prize fighter.

We took turns holding her forehead and rinsing out the pan. We called the hospice nurse, who came and provided medication to help ease nausea. Her belly was swelling with fluid again despite the drainage tube alongside her. The nurse asked if we could bring Sue into the hospital to drain it thoroughly and help relieve the pain. We eventually called an ambulance, and she was painstakingly moved to a gurney and taken to the hospital.

The medical staff was trained, of course, not to stare. But the faces of other patients and their families gave it away, and so did the lingering pat on Sue's hand by one of the nurses. A familiar person passed us in the hallway. It was the head of the cancer department. "You gave Sue renewed trust in doctors," I wanted to say. "We are so grateful to you. And how is your wife? And how are you handling the fears of cancer in your family?" I wanted to hug him and bombard him with all these questions. But he was walking briskly onto his next mission with other younger doctors.

Back home again, Susie's physical world continued to shrink from needing the wheelchair to needing assistance with bathroom needs. Sue had asked for a trapeze for her bed to help her get out. Soon after getting it, she pretended to be a trapeze artist, grinning as she clutched it in her hands and pretended to swing through the air. Again, I tried to smile, amazed that Sue could see the humor even in this. But the day came when she reached for it and couldn't grasp it. Like a cat batting at a ribbon, Sue couldn't get it within her grasp. The honor roll student asked why she couldn't do this simple task. There wasn't medical evidence that cancer had spread to her brain, but we all knew this was possible.

"How we approach death is going to depend upon our fear of life, how much we participated in that life, and how willing we are to let go of this known expression to venture into a new one," was the sentence in a booklet that hospice staff gave to us. "Fear and unfinished business are two big factors in determining how much resistance we put into meeting death."

We moved a beautiful watercolor from the kitchen into her bedroom so she could see it. It showed billowy clouds and an early-spring Midwestern landscape preparing to burst into greenery after awakening from a winter slumber. It could be a focal point, like what we mothers-to-be learned about in our Lamaze class. Concentrating on that could help with bone pain.

Then came the day Sue no longer wanted to read. A book had always been an appendage to my sister, from fairy tales to horse books, to classics, to mysteries, to books on gardening and astronomy. I offered to read to Sue, but that practice was short-lived. Concentration was just too hard to come by.

Mom, Soz, and I visited Sue regularly. Each of us tried to figure out how to be a reservoir of calm and hope while struggling to be in this otherworldly place of being unable to cure Sue. We needed to take turns walking outside to hear the normal sounds of birds chirping as they returned from their wintering grounds.

We also read a book recommended by the hospice staff helped. *Final Gifts: Understanding the Special Awareness, Needs and Communications of the Dying* by Maggie Callahan and Patricia Kelley, 1992. They were two hospice nurses who'd tended to the terminally ill for more than a decade. "When someone we love is dying … it's hard to know how to help, what to do, what to say. Yet if we know how to listen and what to look for, the dying themselves can often supply the answers, letting us know what they need to hear and express to allay their fears and face death with serenity."

It included heart-wrenching yet vital information. The authors wrote about the need for reconciliation and acknowledgment that our loved one's life had made a difference. That was reassuring to read since we unknowingly had done that by team writing "A Prayer for Our Susan." But the bottom line of the book was far too challenging to grasp. At some point, we were supposed to tell our loved ones that it was all right for them to leave this world. *Not going to happen,* I thought, clenching my jaw.

Sue insisted that Mom and I return home for Christopher's eleventh birthday on May 6. He wanted to go to the Japanese steak house to watch them juggle sharp knives and slice, dice, ignite, and sizzle his food. It was the first year after his grandpa Jim had died on May 1. ("I'll never be able to enjoy May Basket Day again," he declared that year.) Young Christopher had seen how frail his aunt Sue was at Easter. But he was such a good-hearted trooper. We never stopped proclaiming, "This is the day the Lord has made; let us rejoice in it!" every day, even as our hearts were breaking.

We followed wise Susan's advice to stay in the present and celebrate Christopher Lovell coming into this world.

When we returned to Sue and Kevin's house, hospice staff gave us booklets that explained the physical signs of someone nearing death.

Clearing the Clutter

There were only narrow pathways available for walking in some parts of Sue and Kevin's house because of unpacked boxes from their move. Unpacking everything just wasn't the priority at a time when precious energy needed to be conserved. And Sue enjoyed the process of projects almost more than the final result, so I restrained myself and waited until Sue wanted a helper. But she no longer had the energy to unpack. I had a nagging thought that Sue should at least be able to sit in her uncluttered living room and enjoy the special touches she'd designed for the house.

Around midnight one night after Sue had settled in, I asked Kevin to help me move and unpack the boxes. Finally, at about 4:00 a.m., we finished. We brought Sue out in her wheelchair that morning. "Oh, it's so beautiful," she said in a strained and barely audible voice. Sue could again look closely at the beautiful hand-built stone fireplace she had designed. She could again see her whimsical forest critter tiles in the kitchen. She waved her hand while saying her thanks.

Sue enjoyed beautiful things, especially antiques. Antiques were appealing because they came with histories and were handcrafted by artisans who'd learned the tradition from those before them. Sue thoroughly researched anything before purchasing and had incredible retention about it all. She and Mom shared their love of antiques as well as books. And, like Mom, sometimes these things became replacements to fill a void for Sue.

Another vital clarification followed the physical clearing of the boxes. Sue told Hedi that she could let go of worrying about her possessions. It's not that she hadn't wanted to share—she was always very generous about sharing everything, from her time, to her possessions, to her money. But now, her possessions no longer represented her value. She had debated a few years back whether she should once again buy an average, practical, high-mileage, economical car or splurge. "Part of me wants something extravagant, just to show me and the world that I'm valuable," she wrote in an email. "And part of me wants to be very practical." So, yes, she went with practical.

But now, she concluded that she no longer needed possessions to feel valuable or to fill a void. Instead, she could now feel the embrace of love.

Soon, she stopped talking. We never expected this. We assumed she would always be able to tell us what she needed and what she was thinking.

Mom and Soz headed back to the motel for the night. Everyone was exhausted. I stayed in the extra bedroom at Sue's, as I had done the past few nights, just in case she needed additional help. Kevin always stayed with Sue on the hospital bed.

But tonight, something was different. Kevin asked me to come into the room. Our Susie wanted company; she wanted to talk.

"I love you guys," she said.

We love you, Susie, so much.

We thanked Sue for her kind, wise, thoughtful approach to life. We reminded her of the difference she had made to many people and four-legged critters. We promised Sue we would try to follow her example. We would try to be more present in the moment. We would try to listen with our hearts and not just our minds to understand what our family and friends truly were telling us.

We would try to live our days on earth thoughtfully instead of just forging ahead mindlessly. We would care about protecting plant and animal diversity on our planet and help teach others to do so. We would respect and honor those who came before us. We would love and care for each other.

The hospice staff had told us it was important to tell our loved one that moving on to the next place is okay. Of course, we didn't want our Sue to be in pain anymore. But to let her go? We hugged and hugged each other. And then hugged again. Sue was quiet, and at some point, she went to sleep.

Prayers and more prayers.

Kevin and I lay on the floor like pet dogs at their master's bedside. We had no sense of time. We each lay with one eye open like first-time moms with newborns, listening for breathing.

Saturday morning dawned. We heard the creak of the front door. Mom and Soz had returned. The hospice staff came to check on things. Hedi came to be with Sue.

Miracles

Sunday was Mother's Day.

On Mother's Day in the Midwest, the weather could be tempestuous, shifting from a bright, balmy day to a dreary, cold one.

We awoke to a breezy, overcast day. I hoped we could all sit outside in the sun a bit, but that would not happen. Saturday night had been a restless, turbulent night. I had been praying for a miracle for our dear Susie. I woke up hugging one of Sue's feather-light down comforters, clutching it like a child with her teddy bear.

I walked into Sue's room and waved good morning. The wind had picked up. I thought about the migrating warblers and worried about them facing such a torrent on the final leg of their trip. I opened the curtains and looked outside Sue's window and saw a sight I had never seen before: the front yard was swarming with dark blue barn swallows, busily darting back and forth and back and forth, like the hand of a mother deftly sewing a button back onto a shirt. They weren't singing. They weren't trying to build nests. Instead, it was a frenzied dance.

While the others did their morning things, I asked Sue if it would be okay to lie next to her. "I think there will be a miracle today," I said softly. I started reading out loud to Sue, then stopped. Stillness, side by side, was much better. My breathing slowed and deepened along with my sister's breath. I patted her hand. "I love you." We breathed slowly together for hours. The swallows circled outside, engrossed in their swooping.

Mom wanted time on this Mother's Day afternoon with her second-born child, Susan Kay, the first baby of the new year, born January 3, 1954, in Mason City, Iowa. She gently laid her hand on Sue's forehead and kissed her, like she had done when we were sick as children. Then she settled into the chair at the foot of Sue's bed with a book. Both Mom and Sue were voracious readers. As adults, they shared a newfound love of mysteries.

Kevin checked to be sure the morphine tubes were in place. We had assumed that Sue would always be able to tell us exactly what she needed, but she could no longer talk.

I glanced at the Sunday newspaper lying on the table. President Bush had already announced aboard the USS *Abraham Lincoln* that primary combat operations had ended in Iraq. Cleanup was happening in Pierce City, Missouri, following a deadly tornado, one of a record number that month. There was a Mother's Day feature story.

Mom came out to say that Sue had gotten restless and suddenly uncomfortable. Kevin gave her more painkillers. Sue had never wanted so much morphine that she would not be aware of her surroundings. Kevin gave her as much as we were allowed to give her. He called the nurses to come and provide an increased dose. But it was Mother's Day and Sunday, and the limited staff was busy. "We will do our best," was the reply.

Mom was massaging Sue's feet. We tried to help Sue think of peaceful memories. "Think of the lake and how it shimmers in the sunlight. You are riding Riffy now, cantering through the field. You are on your bike, pedaling past the woods and now by the prairie. Oh, dear sweet Susie, we love you! Dear God, dear sweet Jesus, please hold and help our brave Susan. Dear God …" And then, it seemed to me that Jesus had led a semicircle of people into the room, their arms outstretched, gently swaying as if in a graceful dance. They were beckoning, welcoming our dear Susie into their dance …

And then there was silence. Prayers. Tears. Hugs. Tears. And more silence.

The funeral home staff solemnly entered with their cart and a black bag. I hadn't watched when they'd taken away my grandma and dad. But I couldn't leave this time. One more hug. One more kiss. They zipped the bag.

It was dark by now, and the funeral home staff looked like silhouettes as they put Susie into the hearse. We all stood there as the hearse began its slow descent down the long, winding driveway, the brake lights flashing on and off in the night.

"Susie!" I wailed, and each of us called her name out loud. We stood in a circle at the top of the long, winding driveway and held one another. There was no wind. There were no swallows.

Be Still and Know

"She was one of the most extraordinary human beings I've known," Hedi said at her memorial service. "I don't mean because of her accomplishments, which were many. But simply because of the kind of person she was. Like all of us, she struggled with the challenges of life. She had disappointments with others and about herself; she had concerns and inner conflicts, sometimes wishing she was more, wanting to contribute more to the planet and humanity.

"What I saw in Susan was her bright light, her deep caring, her ability to love unselfishly, her genuineness, her unusual high intelligence and curiosity, her persistence and patience with those who did not always realize the gifts she offered. She was unassuming and generous in all ways, especially with those in need. She had tremendous compassion."

A friend wrote in a sympathy card:

Dear Kevin,

I've been meaning to write you for quite some time, to put in words my thoughts about Sue and the legacy she left in my life. And legacy is truly the word.

From the day Sue and I met collecting seeds in the same row at (the plant nursery), we clicked. I've found that it's rare to have that feeling, so it's a precious gift when one does …

Her strength was astounding in the days and years that followed [the diagnosis]. She wouldn't let the cancer stop her from wanting and striving to embrace all that she could of life—from immersing herself in remodeling your new home with its proximity to water, its trees and the effigy mounds she loved, to putting out the welcome mat for friends who were stopping by. Sue had this knack to always turn the conversation around to focus on the other person. Having a friend who makes me feel heard is something I cherish, and I am thankful to Sue for having been that for me.

Sue's enduring legacy to me is her model for living a good life. I'll always remember her intelligence and insightfulness, her compassion for others and her sense of justice, her goodness, her independent spirit, her love of and commitment to our environment. But the two things I will remember most are Sue's laughter and her curiosity about everything.

The outpouring of love and kindness helped buoy us.

We can't pretend that we're not heartbroken, Susie. But, as you asked us, we never gave up hope. Thank you, dear Sue, for putting up with the treatments, the discomfort, and the pain to give us all more time together. Thank you for retaining gratitude in the midst of it all, whether it was just for the smell of food because you couldn't eat it after treatments or whether it was for the sound of sandhill cranes returning to Madison. We would never have had enough time with you.

We will always see you as someone who can scale the mountaintops. We hope your example will help us lead our lives more fully. We will try to keep focused on what you told us life is all about. It's about getting along with one another, about learning forgiveness. It's about loving one another.

To Everything, There Is a Season

And then the public grief sharing is over, and the survivors are left to sort out their new normal.

The hospice staff counseled that we may be living in a dream. Understand that you may have irrational thoughts. You may swing between deep sorrow, bottomless regrets, and fierce anger. It's all part of the grieving process.

There were many ways to ride the roller coaster of emotions in those weeks and months following Sue's passing. Some days, I worked intensely to stop the bombardment of what-if questions. Other days, I lay on a hillside at our farm and looked for a sign that our dear Sue was all right. Sometimes I got on a bike and pedaled as hard as possible, as fast as possible, to help wash some anger and sadness away.

Some days, I couldn't even climb aboard the roller coaster.

I worried about our son, who had just turned eleven before Sue passed on. I worried about my mom, who had lost her husband and now her daughter, all within about a year. How could I fathom a mother's grief at losing a child? We read devotions together and hung out together. After Mom passed away, I found the many small pieces of paper she had torn out of her little spiral-bound notebook. She had jotted down things that Sue had said, like, "I feel more powerful than ever before." I worried about Sarah and our nephew Erik and if they were talking about their feelings. I worried about Kevin. While away at college, he'd received a phone call that his older brother had been in a traffic accident. Before he could reach the hospital, his brother had passed away, plummeting Kevin into grief. I worried about my husband worrying about me. I worried about depressing my friends who were trying to comfort me.

I prayed a lot, thinking about my grandmother telling me about the power of prayer.

I went out to the woods and thanked God for Susie. I tried not to think about how she would have enjoyed that glorious day.

We all tried to be more thoughtful in our actions and toward one another. We tried to love more, forgive more, and spend more time with family.

I found notes that I had written while at Sue and Kevin's:

Sue would have:
Loved more
Forgiven more
Been closer to her family

Priorities changed. The debate over previously important things no longer deserved the time. "Is it a matter of life or death?" was my new standard. If not, don't sweat it.

We channeled our energy into projects that would honor Sue. Kevin busied himself removing buckthorn, Sue's invasive plant nemesis, from their yard. He helped on prairie restoration projects in Madison. We continued to fundraise in the Walk and Run for the Cure. We contributed to breast cancer research. I decided to participate in the National Institute of Health Sister Study for those who have sisters diagnosed with breast cancer.

But it was hard. It was so hard. *God's love, God's love, God's love,* we all reminded one another. *That is what will get us through.*

"Grieving the death of a loved one is a normal and necessary process," was noted in a letter from a hospice in north Iowa. "Most of us are not prepared for the long journey of grief, which is sometimes devastating, other times frightening, and often lonely. Grieving is a process that takes time—a person does not simply 'get over it.' Remember, there are no easy answers or shortcuts, no way under, over, or around grief. Although grief may hurt desperately, we must go through it."

I thought it might help to write about the experience as a way to grapple with it. So I attended a workshop by a writer whose books were meaningful to me. After the presentation, I went up to ask her a question. "You need more joy in your life," the best-selling author said to me before I could ask.

Excuse me? I thought with a jolt. *Is it* that *obvious?*

I tend to rehash what I should have done and how I failed to see what was happening. But a perfect stranger telling me what I need?

So how do we find that wellspring of joy again?

Restoration

With the new energy of summer, we worked on mapping out the prairie and wetlands restoration and reconstruction at the family farm.

Ironically, we were undoing the backbreaking work of our ancestors and other immigrants who had discovered the miraculous productivity of the rich prairie soil. After the glaciers retreated from Iowa over ten thousand years ago, the prairie took hold next with its grasses, forbs, and deep root systems. Raging prairie fires burned dead material off the top of the plants and returned nutrients to the earth, resprouting plants from the deep roots. Layer by layer and thousands of years later, this interdependent ecosystem created the fertile black soils of Iowa. This environment sustained plentiful wildlife and Native Americans.

But Iowa's landscape changed dramatically with the advent of the plow and waves of European immigrants eager to make a new life in America. Settlers painstakingly hand-dug tiles to drain wetlands and fenced in the seemingly endless sea of prairie. As a result, Iowa had the most transformed landscape of any state in the nation in less than a generation. Today, less than 0.1 percent of Iowa's native prairies remain.

Now, scientists are helping us understand the importance of having a balance. Wetlands, for example, provide a natural filter for soil and chemical runoff from surrounding farmland into the glacially carved Clear Lake. Iowa's many rivers can receive water quality benefits from natural riparian buffers. Restored floodplains can save millions of dollars in preventing destruction. Prairies help sequester carbon. Humans and other living creatures need some natural habitat for our well-being.

Sue understood that need for balance long ago.

Like master chefs selecting just the right ingredients for a culinary masterpiece, we took great care to achieve just the right prairie seed mixture. We tapped the expertise of the Iowa Natural Heritage Foundation staff and the Natural Resources Conservation Service. The seeds would become an undulating sea of prairie color, from the early bloomers of prairie smoke and prairie phlox in April and May to the black-eyed Susans in June and July and the asters in late season. While it could not have the divine design of native prairie, the goal was to reconstruct a prairie and wetlands ecosystem that reflected original flora as much as possible. That meant using prairie seeds collected from nearby native prairie remnants to reinvite the red fox, badger, and other prairie critters to this new home. Our goal was for it to become a destination for migrating monarch butterflies, bald eagles, and neotropical birds trekking the Mississippi River flyway. We also worked with other groups to design a bike and walking path that meanders through the prairie to help awaken people to this native beauty in their backyards.

Soon, the sun-kissed days of a Midwest autumn disappeared as the blaze of golden and red leaves began to blanket the ground. The first large burlap bags of native prairie seed were delivered and placed in an empty silo, creating a sweet and ancient aroma. After the final harvest of soybeans, the ground was ready for the return of the prairie and wetlands. And new life.

Milkweed pods in the nearby pasture were bursting open, and their silken filaments carried playfully in the wind to plant seeds elsewhere. I walked over to take a closer look. Some dismiss the common milkweed here as a lowly weed because of its name and dull, coarse pod. But we Connell sisters had always delighted in seeing the feathery, silken strands in shimmering overlapping rows intermingled with seeds. The milkweed is the host plant of monarch butterflies and a critical piece in their long migration journey. Others have been drawn to this plant, as botanists placed it in the genus *Asclepias*, named after Asclepius, the god of medicine and healing in ancient Greek mythology.

A gentle wind lifted the silken strands from my hand, away across the pasture. It was a fairyland-like scene, with silky strands spreading their promise of new life. I brought one back to Mom and told her about the experience. Like the milkweed, Sue was sowing seeds of love, knowledge, and forgiveness to those around her. "We can't cling too tightly," I said. We could no more cling to our dear Sue than the milkweed could prevent its pod from opening. "To let things grow, we need to let it go."

By the time all the seeds had arrived, it was after Thanksgiving. That was very late in the year to consider planting, and the local professional thought it too risky. But Joe McGovern from the Iowa Natural Heritage Foundation had faith in the timing and the seed diversity.

Dan, a young man from the prairie restoration company, explained how he would broadcast the seed and smooth the seedbed with a cultipacker. He broadly smiled as he talked about how much he loved his work and helping nudge some of the earth back into balance. "The ground is still soft and receptive to seed," Dan said.

After a few days of work, he had just one final section. "Some snow is forecasted for tonight," he noted, climbing aboard the tractor. "That's okay, though," Dan said, "because that moisture will help ensure the wind won't blow the seed away."

He continued seeding into the night, and we watched the small headlight from his vehicle traversing across the field. Soon, light snow began to fall, creating a tender blanket on the dormant earth to store energy for new life and the next great migration.

Jan

As a little girl, I loved to walk into church and see the large, colorful picture of children surrounding a smiling Jesus. They were kids from all over the world—a boy from the African bush, a Dutch girl wearing wooden shoes, another from China, plus a blond-haired, blue-eyed girl. That had to be me. Jesus was looking with kindness and love as He walked with us along a path that disappeared in the distance.

I could not have imagined then that the gentle path also would include rugged mountains and deep valleys with twists and hairpin turns, raging rivers to cross, and some gut-wrenching experiences along the way.

I was the third daughter of three girls. And yes, it was not unusual for a grown-up to comment, "Three girls! Your poor parents!" when they met us.

So why in the world would I begin to think that my story would be of interest to anyone? I'm not famous. I grew up in the flyover country of Iowa, and I'm a Caucasian woman with no exotic ethnic background information—although there is some unconfirmed information that a few of our Irish ancestors may have dabbled in some piracy …

I'm just on a life journey like you. But apparently I need to experience life events numerous times before I get it. So while we are each unique, perhaps there are some nuggets from my story to help others along this journey.

Our backyard was a lake, which provided an integral backdrop to seasonal outdoor activities while growing up. Best of all were family picnics in the woods on the south side of the lake. We imagined ourselves as intrepid adventurers as we explored, discovered wildflowers, or saw a whitetail deer in the distance. Unfortunately, my gram had extensive arthritis, so she could not walk with us. But she told stories about how her aunt Janet taught her about native wildflowers and to identify birdsongs as they hiked along the shoreline. It provided a tangible, comforting sense of knowing our place in the natural cycle.

My grandparents exemplified solid Midwestern values of hard work and family. My grandfather, the son of Norwegian immigrants, served his country as a World War I medic in France instead of completing college. He returned to Clear Lake to open his first of several grocery stores he would own across the region.

War also helped define my parents' relationship. After my dad served in World War II, he stayed in the army reserve to earn extra money. He met my mom while they were both college students; they married and eventually moved to Clear Lake. But then the Korean conflict flared, and he was called back to serve. As a result, he was leading an infantry rifle platoon in Korea when my parents' first child was born.

They never talked about it, at least with us. But the stress of one spouse being in combat half a world away and the other being a single parent, praying that her husband would return alive, isn't part of any young family's plan.

Then, two more children, all three close in age. It was a busy, hectic time for my parents. Dad worked long hours. Mom had her hands full, raising us and keeping our household up to that generation's standard. There was little discussion about anyone's day because we ate so late. Afterward, we each headed off to our respective rooms to study.

I think we were good kids overall, but we had our moments. "Spare the rod and spoil the child" was the accepted physical discipline theory of the time. And we were expected to follow the rules—no questions. My dad was the fourth of six kids, so I assume he got the belt. But that didn't make it any less terrifying. Sometimes we all got yardstick thwacks right away. The worst was when we would hear, "Wait 'til your father gets home!" Mom sent each of us to our rooms to sit alone and await punishment, sometimes for hours. Eventually, we would hear Dad's footsteps coming up the stairs. There would be angry words, the sound of the thick wooden yardstick, and a sister's cries. Do I run into the room and plead for it to stop? Next, the same would happen in my other sister's room. *Thwack!* More sobbing. And finally, my door opened. I would grit my teeth. Why would they want to hurt us?

Maybe that contributed to my fierce compassion for the little guy, for justice for the downtrodden. Perhaps that was why I was attracted to books like *Beautiful Joe* and *Black Beauty*, which brought awareness to animal cruelty and the need for compassion and trust between owner and animal during training. I had already seen our pets' nonjudgmental, faithful love toward us.

Like so many families in those days, we were regular attendees at church. I loved cuddling next to my gram and reading the exciting Sunday Pix and the stories of how my favorite character would courageously stand up for Christians against the bad guys. Confirmation was meaningful because our leader let us ask questions and have a discussion.

I was a junior high schooler in the 1960s when our country faced major turmoil of Vietnam War protests, government corruption, race riots, and Martin Luther King Jr. and Bobby Kennedy gunned down in cold blood. The youth rebelled against the older generation by growing long hair and wearing miniskirts. The traditional church was in transformation, and TV evangelist scandals made headlines.

I participated in many school organizations and activities and got mainly good grades. But I yearned for adventure, and the summer before my senior year, I signed up for a three-week experience of backpacking, whitewater canoeing, orienteering, and rock climbing. It was named Vanguards for a reason—they would test our mettle, leadership skills, and, ultimately, our faith. Soon after arrival, we learned that our adult leaders would be silent followers. So it was up to us high schoolers to use a map and compass (pre-GPS) to find our way across northern Wisconsin and Michigan, through bogs and woodlands, with little food and scant fresh water.

The last challenge was to camp alone on the shores of Lake Superior. Each girl, exhausted, bug-bitten, and hungry, found her campsite and was given a bottle of water, a tarp, a sleeping bag, and a pen and paper to journal her thoughts. We had twenty-four hours to contemplate our experience.

After setting up "camp," I watched the sun set over Lake Superior. As darkness crept in, I jotted down some of the lessons I had learned: there are many things in our lives that we cannot control; we can accomplish so much more by working together; we each had an inner strength that we had not recognized. I hoped I boosted my confidence to help others after doing the ropes-course test, backpacking, and rappelling down a rugged cliff in the Porcupine Mountains. I also wrote:

> I just sat and watched with awe at the magnificence of God's creation. How tremendous and loving He must be to create such beauty for us to see in nature and people.
>
> I know I have a definite purpose in life for God and that God has given me a choice in what to do. I pray to Him to help me understand His plan.
>
> Most importantly, I learned that God provides no matter how difficult the situation. That glorious sunset was a reminder of Who is in charge.

That experience was a launching pad for college adventures. I wanted to be a journalist, so I joined the college newspaper staff. My editor assigned me to write primarily frothy feature stories, but there were a few of substance. For example, I interviewed a South Vietnamese student whose family had narrowly escaped their home city of Saigon just before the North Vietnamese captured it. I rewrote that article numerous times as I wrestled with the paramount responsibility of a journalist to factually convey this fellow college freshman's dramatic story.

While at college, my friend Tom and I started getting serious about each other. We had some dates in high school, but we had also dated others, and he went to college in another state. While there, he almost died from a ruptured appendix. His dad had died from a misdiagnosis of appendicitis, so this incident hit home. Our relationship deepened. He allowed himself to grieve deeply—maybe for the first time —as he told me how hard it was as a fifth-grade boy never to see his father again after he left for the emergency room. We had many conversations about our faith and enjoyed outdoor activities together. I enjoyed hearing him sing and play his guitar. And then he composed a song about us.

Okay—there goes my heart.

When Tom started getting law school information, I encouraged him to consider applying to schools in other parts of the country, like Portland, Oregon. It had a great law school and undergraduate college and was equidistant from outdoor adventures in the ocean, mountains, and rivers. He was going to be an environmental lawyer; I was going to be a reporter for a metro newspaper after graduation.

Westward ho!

I transferred to a college in Portland, joined the newspaper staff, and got to write the local perspective of some international stories, including an interview with Iranian students regarding the Shah of Iran's political unrest and reporting on protests over the

South African prime minister's visit and his country's abhorrent apartheid system of racial segregation.

After college graduation and our wedding and honeymoon, we packed up, said goodbye to our families, and headed west to our new home in Oregon. I had built up a résumé of freelance work during college to help land my first newspaper job; Tom would finish his last year of law school. After that, the world was our oyster!

Once we arrived in Portland, I stopped at a pay phone (no cell phones back then) to tell my folks we were safe and sound. But my parents hemmed and hawed—was something wrong? "We have terrible news," they said. "Your grandfather had a massive stroke yesterday." He worked in the garden on that hot July day, returned to the house, and suddenly collapsed. And he was in critical condition.

How could this be happening with my high-energy Gramp? We just talked with each other about the fun of the wedding. Tom and I just got out here to start a life together, and suddenly, my beloved Gramp is deathly ill?

I hurriedly packed a suitcase, and my husband took me to the airport. Staring out the window at the clouds below on the way to Minneapolis, I remembered Gramp saying, "When you have your health, you have everything."

I hoped I would make it in time.

I returned to see my grandpa lying in the hospital bed attached to multiple monitors and tubes, his slight smile off-kilter from paralysis. He tried to speak, but I just gently patted his hand. My sisters, Gram, Mom, and Dad had been at his hospital bedside. I was so grateful he survived the stroke, but soon reality started to sink in. Suddenly, he could no longer walk alone, speak clearly, or feed himself. He would get physical therapy to help recover, but it would be a long time in the nursing home with physical therapy before returning home.

After he stabilized in the nursing home, the three sisters headed back to their homes. An expression kept running through my head on the trip back to Portland. *Everything can change in the blink of an eye. So forgive often and love with all your heart.*

We had a part-time job as managers of a small apartment complex in Oregon, so there were toilets to unplug, cleaning and repairs to do, and some squabbles to help referee. More importantly, I needed full-time employment, and Tom was preparing to dive into his final year of law school. Thankfully, I was hired as a general assignment reporter at a Portland, Oregon, suburban newspaper and earned my stripes covering contentious meetings in a rapidly growing area. "If you can't stand the heat, get out of the kitchen," one editor quipped.

But as much as we enjoyed Oregon, it became apparent that we spent our limited vacations traveling back to the Midwest to see our families. So ultimately, we said goodbye to friends and Oregon outdoor adventures and moved to St. Paul, Minnesota, and I got a job at a Twin Cities suburban newspaper. Next stop, Tom got a job as an assistant county attorney, and I was the city-beat reporter in Red Wing, a newsy Mississippi River town. Then, a few years later, Tom was offered the opportunity to join his stepfather's law office back in our hometown. Unfortunately, my Gramp never fully recovered from that stroke and passed away a few years later. Gram had been living alone since then, so this was a chance to help keep her company and hopefully work at the area's daily newspaper.

Soon I was back in another newsroom with its stereotypical crusty editors and doing general assignment reporting and in-depth stories. I loved the variety of assignments, the people I met, and the fascinating puzzle of transforming random information into something meaningful. But the late shift caused my hubby and I to be ships passing in the night. We wanted to start a family. Plus, it became clear that if anyone from our generation was going to be active in the family telecommunications business, this was the time. I like to learn new things, but I'm not a stereotypical bottom-line businessperson. *So is this what I am going to be* as *I grow up?*

To learn the business, I got on-the-job training alongside each employee and read industry textbooks at night. Later, I enrolled in a master's degree telecommunications graduate program in Minneapolis and did my thesis on strategic planning. I enjoyed our team and their families and wanted to help them prosper. I had worked for enough other bosses that I set a goal of fostering a positive workplace environment. Its foundation would include the golden rule of respectful treatment, personal development, and having fun while working together for a common purpose. Federal deregulation and ever-changing technology ensured that the job would never be dull. Plus, we could provide state-of-the-art technology so our small town could attract and retain industries and jobs, or people could enjoy life here and telecommute to a corporate job elsewhere. Donating at a business level to worthy causes was also appealing.

Those were my bottom lines.

I also was grateful to be able to help Gram, converse about growing up in the early 1900s, work on scrapbooks together, and share chuckles. Common threads in our wide-ranging discussions were Gram's lifelong tenets—"Treat others like you want to be treated," "Put yourself in the other person's shoes," and "Your faith will carry you through." Her daily life exemplified them all.

Sadly, within just a few years of moving back, Gram was diagnosed with congestive heart failure. I had a difficult time grasping the possibility of losing Gram. But when I shared my fear of losing her, she reminded me to focus on being grateful for the time we could spend together. All too soon, Gram passed on.

One of my wide-ranging conversations with Gram was about my "never enough" concerns, this time about me becoming a parent. With her gentle, you'll-be-just-fine-Janny tone of voice, she told me that many worry about falling short as parents. But she cherished being a mother; it was a gift from God. Tom echoed those sentiments, and years later, our prayers were answered. We were expecting a baby. Thank You, God.

Like most expectant new parents, we had a lot to learn. Since many of my friends had passed the baby stage, I read every baby and child development book I could get my hands on. One standout book was *Whole Child / Whole Parent* by Polly Berrien Berends, HarperCollins, 1975. While the other books presented specific stages, this author's premise was that life is a journey of spiritual awakening from childhood through adulthood. Society expects that getting married and having a baby is part of fulfilling ourselves and becoming whole. But instead, the author posited that having children becomes a journey of both parent and child awakening to what makes each of us whole—God's love. "Parenthood is just about the world's most intensive course in love," she wrote. "We are not parents merely to give or get love but to discover love as the fundamental fact of life and the truth of our being and thus bring it into expression."

While awaiting the birth, I wrote in the "Dreams for Our Baby" section of our baby book. I hoped our baby would live a joyous life of purpose and have compassion for those in need. I hoped our child would always know the assurance of parental love and, more importantly, of God's everlasting love.

When it was finally time for this long-awaited baby to be born, I wasn't deterred by the mother-to-be's screams as we entered the hospital maternity ward. My soothing music helped for about ten minutes, and then it was time to focus. When the same nurse I met Monday said, "You are still here?" on Wednesday, I wearily waved.

But all that vanished when I cradled this precious baby boy in my arms and kissed his head for the first time. It's impossible to describe the outpouring of love encircling us as I looked into his face and felt his breath while we cuddled.

Does this give us an inkling of how the Creator feels about His children?

Oh sure, Tom and I were in the baby fog, as a good friend called it. Tom was a great hands-on dad. I slept with one eye open and was a walking zombie since we did not have much of a sleep or feeding schedule. But, oh my—the joy and excitement of all the firsts. The miracle of recognizing voices and faces, the first smile, laugh, and hug. And then, stages of playing make-believe, rolling a ball, riding a bike, and much more—each extensively documented with photographs and journals.

Soon we received the lessons of love from our little one. Our son was looking at his Little Children's Worship Bulletin, titled "When you do something good for someone, God shows through you!" There was a space to draw a picture of himself with someone he made feel happy. So Christopher drew a picture of a boy and his mom and titled it "My Mommy Because I Love Her." *Thank You, God, for this incredible blessing.*

We all rejoiced when my oldest sister and her husband had their son about a year later. We looked forward to the boys growing up together, trips, family get-togethers, and lots of fun times with both sets of grandparents, aunts and uncles, and cousins.

Life Is What Happens When You're Making Plans

✓ college education
✓ job
✓ marriage
✓ starting our family

Sister is diagnosed with metastatic breast cancer.

PART II

What's Next?
It Is a Choice.

So, what do we do next?

What do you do after you help your mom and brother-in-law dress your sister's lifeless body in the final outfit she'd asked to wear?

What do you do after you give her a final kiss before they zip up the body bag?

What do you do as the hearse slowly pulls away and winds down the long driveway, its brake lights flashing on and off before disappearing into the darkness?

"Suuuuusieeeeeeee!" I cried as we all stood at the top of the driveway.

We stood speechless, staring in disbelief into the night. We all hugged.

How do I comfort my mom, who just lost her daughter? What words of comfort can I give Kevin or our son or my sister Sarah? What do I do in this sudden, stark, deathly silent, new reality without our Susie, without my sister?

After all of Sue's suffering, treatments, and praying earnestly for a miracle, it's now over.

What next, dear God?

Or what next for Mary after hearing that her daughter had taken her life? Or what next for Craig after the doctor tells him he has a terminal disease? How do we handle life's inevitable losses—the death of our loved ones, tragedies, disease, war, conflict, and shattered dreams?

Sadness, denial, shock, despair, confusion, and anger are all part of the grieving process that can last for what seems like forever, then disappear, only to reappear. Such pain. So surreal.

I knew that Sue was no longer suffering and was at peace. Yet I still slipped back into the same futile questions of "Why didn't I do this? Why didn't I do that?" and so on. I wanted a recipe, a formula, and a mentor to give me instructions. Sue had been a great cook. I needed her recipe to heal our broken hearts.

Yet Kevin and I had sworn to Sue in her final days that we would try to live more thoughtfully and with a greater love for our families and others and that we would try to be better, kinder people to make a positive difference in the world.

As Sue and others in these stories demonstrated with their lives, we can choose to forgive and love more and start and end each day with gratitude. We can walk alongside one another for support. We can share the insight we have learned from our experiences. We can choose to work toward leaving the world a better place.

Some say the bottom line is whether people should live for their résumé or their obituary. Living for one's résumé denotes accomplishments and specific skills. Living for one's obituary focuses on emotional contribution, commitment, and legacies.

While their specific circumstances differed, Mary, Craig, Hedi, Mary Ann, and Sue each chose to live fully and compassionately instead of becoming embittered by their pain.

While on this journey, there are choices we can make. So who do you want to be *as* you grow up? A kinder, more compassionate person? Someone who leaves the world a better place? Someone who doesn't judge others?

But first, you must acknowledge the emotional roller coaster you have been on and start slowly.

Just Breathe

My first response to a stressful situation tends to be to stop breathing, grit my teeth, and tense up into a tight bundle.

That doesn't help.

It is a punch in the gut to lose a loved one, be dealing with your child's cancer treatments, or be in any storm that launched you into the unknown, turbulent waters.

Remember to breathe instead of just gritting your teeth or clenching your fists. Be kind to yourself as you try to sort out a new normal.

For those who lost a loved one, know that we each can grieve differently and for varying lengths of time. Rituals in some cultures enable individuals to wear a specific clothing color or have a publicly accepted timeframe for extended grieving to give others a heads-up that someone is in a vulnerable space.

Our culture typically does not allow that leeway, as we expect a quick return to fast-paced living. So it can be tempting to put on a happy face or ignore grief by filling your days with distractions. But your grief experience may not be the same as your best friend's, and it is crucial to go through it. Don't fear extreme ups and downs. Sometimes my grief about my sister Sue was so difficult that I wondered if it would ever lift. But it does, it did, and it will.

If you were a caregiver, you probably put activities with friends on hold, you may not have been eating or sleeping regularly, and your physical world shrank. So all the more reason to give yourself time to get back to healthy habits. There are helpful books and information online from reputable sources. Reach out to support groups and others to help confirm that your feelings are normal.

Pray for God's help in getting through this. It is not easy, even for those with profound faith like Char.

Char's Story

Char is one of those people who wears her love and compassion on her sleeve. With her ever-present smile, bright eyes, and nursing education, we were so grateful that she could help Mom mend from a broken hip. I remember a good friend saying, "She must be an angel."

I agree.

Char's personal story of hardship unfolded just a few pages at a time as we got to know her. As they say, life is what happens while you're making plans.

Char, her husband, Bob, and their four sons were a hardworking, salt-of-the-earth Midwestern family, with everyone busy with school and church activities and farmwork. Bob started to notice mild twitches in his upper arms that got more severe with time. Bob was just forty-seven years old, and their sons ranged in age from ten to twenty. A doctor told them there was a chance it could be amyotrophic lateral sclerosis—ALS or Lou Gehrig's disease. They spent their days praying, crying, eating, and sleeping very little until the subsequent tests. A roller coaster continued for months with doctor visits, tests, waiting and waiting, and many prayers. Then, finally, there was a diagnosis.

"When you are told you have ALS, you go through a devastating period of grief as a whole family," Char said. "It is a death sentence. There are no possibilities of treatment, surgery, or medication. There were lots of tears, but then, by God's grace, we went about the business of living life, trusting God, and doing everything we could humanly do to extend Bob's life."

"We are so thankful to God for His goodness to us over the years," Char wrote in a Christmas letter. "We had many more hopes and dreams and plans as a family ... It is comforting to know that God is in control and that His plan is best, even if we do not understand. We know that He is always near, walking beside us, and when we cannot walk, He will carry us ... We do not know what all lies ahead for us. Each case is different and so even the doctor cannot say for sure. May God give us His grace to face each day."

As part of the disease progression in the first few years, Bob started losing the use of his hands and arms. Char was feeding, dressing, and toileting her husband within a few years. The treatment process was ever changing: he took part in a clinical trial for a potential new ALS treatment, he was fed through an IV, he went on a respirator, then had a tracheotomy, and he had to have his throat suctioned. During this roller-coaster time of so many health changes, two of their sons were seriously injured when a vehicle swung into their lane and collided with them head-on. Thankfully, they fully recovered. Char also cared for her elderly father-in-law and father in their busy home.

Listening to a Christian radio station and CDs kept Char focused on Jesus daily instead of worrying about the future. "God has faithfully supplied us with His grace and peace for each new day," Char wrote in one of her Christmas letters.

Bob's mind remained sharp, so his sons could ask for advice on farming matters, and he could stay attuned to everyone's activities. And they celebrated family members' graduation from high school and college, weddings, and grandbabies' births.

They were also grateful for the opportunity to show other people their sustained love for one another and their faith in God through these hardships. Char noted that they often had that opportunity at doctor's visits, the hospital, and nursing homes. "This has been the silver lining behind the cloud," Char said, thoughtfully adding that they would not have had those chances if Bob hadn't gotten sick.

The following year was a mixture of gratefulness and sadness: Char's dad passed away from cancer, but twin grandchildren who were born prematurely celebrated their first birthdays, and a son got married.

Then Bob's health began a steep decline, despite trying every intervention. Family members were called home as they worked to keep him comfortable and alive. They were grateful for his extra years beyond the doctor's predictions. But they weren't ready for him to leave them.

Herculean efforts ultimately did not prevail, and Bob passed away on September 1. Because it was Labor Day weekend, they waited until September 5 to hold the funeral—which would have been their thirty-second wedding anniversary. Instead, they sang songs of faith as family and friends gathered for the church service and at the cemetery.

It had been an eleven-year journey for Char of lovingly caring for her beloved husband. The loss of him hit hard.

"I had lost my husband, my best friend, and my full-time job," Char wrote in a letter to family and dear friends who lived far away. She had not written a Christmas letter to them for almost seven years. "Nothing in my life was the same."

The following week was the 9/11 terrorist attack on the United States.

> I sat in the recliner next to Bob's empty bed and watched the news for days as tears ran down my face. So many things are now a blur in my mind, but I will not forget that memory or how it felt

to me as if life had stopped, but all around me it kept right on going.

And then after being home for over five years, I could go to church again. That was so difficult. There are no words to explain how it felt to be sitting in our loving, caring church and feeling so incredibly alone. Back at home, I would forget that I could run down to the basement or go into the garage and not have to hurry right back in to listen for the ventilator. The house was so quiet. I had loved Christian radio, and we had listened to it for so many hours every day ... and now I could not even listen to that. Not because I didn't love it but because I couldn't bear that much emotion. A kind friend stopped by and mentioned it was too quiet. I turned on the radio when he left, and it became a comfort and encouragement to me once again, and it still is.

Immediately after Bob died, I had this overwhelming need to talk to him just one more time. After all those years, you would think I would have been ready, but I was not. We had given every ounce of our being into keeping him alive ... but he died. Had I done enough? Had I said the right things? I needed to talk with him about the dying part. It almost became an obsession. I would think about it all day, and then at night I would try to sleep, and I would relive his death.

She felt so sorry for her sons losing their dad and her husband, who wanted so much to live. When she could fall asleep, she would dream he'd returned so she could talk with him one more time.

Soon after her husband died, Char was asked to help rebuild their church's after-school children's outreach ministry. As difficult as it was, she felt that God still had work for her to do. The project was exhilarating and exhausting. Char said that she would not have imagined years ago in her small town the issues that families would be dealing with—drug, alcohol, and sexual abuse, a parent serving time in prison, and more. "We are encouraged and discouraged as people's lives go up and down, but we are thankful that God's faithfulness remains the same," she said.

A friend also asked Char to start working at a local business. It was hard for her to say no but also hard to be there.

> I would think of Bob almost constantly. I soon found out that 99% of the people you meet automatically say, "Hi, how are you?" I had no idea how to answer that so I would smile and say, "Hi, how are YOU?" Those first two years, yes, two whole years, I felt as if I was drowning all the time, as if I couldn't breathe, and yet the whole time I KNEW God would not let me drown and that He had His arms around me. Part way through, I remember thinking, "I don't want to do this anymore," but there is no way to get from point A to point C without going through point B. For two years, I could not sing in the church choir or on the praise team. I could not order the stone for the cemetery and I could not write a Christmas letter.
>
> Then one day in the beginning of the third year I remember I was at work at the pharmacy, counting pills, and I thought to myself, "I'm breathing! I am breathing!" A few days later someone came in and said, "Hi, how are you?"

and I heard myself say, "I'm good, how are you?" I almost startled myself … I had just said "I'm good." Thank you, thank you God. Through it all, it had been a great comfort to know in my heart that even though I was sad, I was not unhappy. All those years of Bob's sickness I had two main prayers: 1. "Heal Bob if that could be your will." (He was healed on Sept. 1) 2. "Lord, I will do anything you ask, but please don't ever let me be bitter." God graciously answered that prayer and I can testify that He has never allowed me to have one minute of anger or bitterness.

In the remainder of the Christmas letter, she writes about how she loves her new job of providing home care, some trips she enjoyed, church work, and being with her family. "I have tried to continue to do what I feel God has wanted me to do," Char said.

Cradle Yourself in God' s Healing Nature

After Sue passed away, there were just two places where I wanted to be—either with my family at home or in the woods. Being out in God's creation is always a reaffirming connection to my Creator. It also reminds me that we are all part of a natural rhythm.

I am just a sister, not a medical doctor, for sure. But I'm convinced that Sue's deep-seated understanding of and appreciation for creation helped extend her days on this earth.

Sue was happiest when she was in sync with the natural world, whether during the hard physical work of prairie restoration, hiking up a mountain, or filling the birdfeeder. Of course, she enjoyed the dramatic landscapes of living in Montana and Colorado. But she especially loved the Midwest's subtle beauty while biking through a prairie, seeing the big sky, or watching a storm front closing in.

Sue was a voracious reader who enjoyed a deep, academic understanding of geology, plant species, and ecosystems. But despite her ability to understand the complexities and interrelationships, she also retained a childlike ability to marvel at creation, a trait that Rachel Carson praised in her groundbreaking book *Silent Spring.* "Those who contemplate the beauty of the earth find reserves of strength that will endure as long as life lasts" (Rachel Carson, *Silent Spring*, Houghton Mifflin, 1962).

After the cancer diagnosis, Sue and Kevin started looking for a different house because of the possible future need for accessibility and bathroom facilities on the ground floor. Plus, that provided a positive goal for focus.

After months of searching, they found it. It was on a deep lot in rural Madison. The long asphalt driveway wound past a wooded area up a hill toward the house. There were Native American mounds, the most visible evidence that the site had long been sacred. Sue loved having the mounds there and was soon researching their history. Native critters, like sandhill cranes and whitetail deer, loved the area. Their backyard was Lake Waubesa, where Sue hoped to kayak.

"We're about to have our first night in the new house ..." Sue faxed on March 19, 2002. "It's very nice, even with all the piles of boxes & garbage bags to go through ... Kevin and I both really like it here! So many more birds to hear & see, so much more of a view, so much more sun & air! It's wonderful!"

Sue's yard and house deck featured a maze of birdfeeders that attracted a diverse winged population. She knew each of their species. She could distinguish their songs. She placed decals on the large picture windows of their house to prevent collisions during migration season. Sue took action to meet that need to connect with nature.

But that need is fundamental to all of us. For example, during the coronavirus global pandemic, natural areas, parks, and bike trails were lifeboats for people cooped up during an extended lockdown or quarantine. The fresh air, the sunshine, and the social distance outside helped counteract the invisible threat and provide a mental escape to relieve the stress.

Even in normal times without a pandemic, where do city dwellers across the globe go to relax? To the park, the beach, the mountains, the cabin in the woods. In Istanbul, Turkey, residents felt so strongly about their park that eight people were killed and thousands injured while protesting the government's plan to develop Gezi Park in Istanbul. This tiny, nine-acre park was one of Istanbul's last central green spaces, where families could enjoy picnics, outdoor games, and strolls among the trees. Government officials in Botswana, Africa decided that instead of destroying natural areas and wildlife, they could ensure that all urban school children take at least one safari trip to experience the wild animal kingdom. That animal kingdom helps sustain the economy as droves of tourists come to photograph animals.

Gardeners can tell you about the life-reaffirming aspect of their outdoor hobby.

I deeply missed my gram when she passed on at age eighty-four from congestive heart failure. One Saturday morning, I wandered over to what used to be my grandparents' garden but had become a forgotten lot across the street. I recalled how happy Gramp looked, wearing his rumpled work shirt, canvas work pants, dirty gloves, and disheveled hair while busily weeding his vast vegetable garden. Then I noticed Gram's peonies blooming.

I decided it would be nice to weed those areas and give them some freedom to grow after all those years. And, as one thing inevitably leads to another, I started planting a few new flowers and, later, some trees. Restoring and renovating that garden became a way to channel my grief physically. There was something primal about digging in the dirt, something hopeful about planting and nurturing growth and springtime miracles.

It unofficially became a Peace Garden, fronting one of the busier streets in this little town. It is available to anyone to enjoy as a place of respite and a haven for migrating birds and butterflies.

Reconnection

When you are ready, reconnect with others to help heal. Reconnection is also a step toward living more fully and fulfilling our potential despite hardships. Because isn't there something within us that intrinsically knows we can be better? Even perennial plants endure harsh temperatures and wildlife nibbling, but they reach for the Light of spring to blossom.

Let's call it our "My Better Self" plan. We each will face storms, but we can choose to become more resilient and more vital through them. Like a workout plan that starts slowly and gradually accelerates to add muscle, the My Better Self plan can be a lifelong plan of choosing to grow and learn.

Lighten Your Heavy Heart by Sharing What You Have Learned

Mary Ehmke experienced a mutual healing process and a heart-to-heart connection when she reached out to other parents who had lost a child. They knew she was someone who truly understood the suffocating depth of pain. And they could see that she had made it through.

Sister Sue created her best practices and used these in conjunction with her oncology team's medical regime. Her methods provided continuity in a world turned upside down, gave her a sense of control, and augmented her medical routine. As an instinctual teacher, she sought opportunities to help anyone with a daunting medical illness. Here are a few of them:

Information Is Power: Instead of avoiding reading breast cancer information for fear of reading something scary, Sue researched it voraciously to understand current research and ask the right questions at her next oncologist appointment.

Our family attended numerous weekend sessions on women's cancers at the famed Mayo Clinic. At everyone's urging, Sue went to the Mayo Clinic for a second opinion to reaffirm her treatment options and to learn about other options. And we heard, numerous times, that *healing* doesn't always mean healing of just the physical body.

More information is available online now than at the time Sue was diagnosed. But be intentional about not being overwhelmed, cautioned a wise friend who survived several bouts with cancer. Know that some of the information you receive will conflict with others. But stay focused on the big picture that your medical team is providing.

Say What You Need: Asserting your needs is okay and essential. Cancer can make one feel like things are out of control, so vocalizing your desires is especially important now. It can be in little things or big things.

Who would have imagined that being too nice would become a matter of life and death? It's important to be kind and polite, but we three daughters were trained that being courteous to others was paramount, no matter what the repercussions for us. Sue said that she should have been a better advocate for herself. Pay attention to your gut instinct and know that even nice people can respectfully disagree with the experts.

Write a Summary for Your Doctor: Rather than stressing about remembering everything that had occurred since her last doctor's appointment, Sue typed up her observations and questions regularly, summarized them, and gave these notes to her doctor to read at the beginning of each meeting.

This "patient update" summarized how she was feeling and what she hoped to get out of her next appointment, including test results, other treatment options, significant questions, current medications, and ways to handle nausea and pain. It gave her some closure on her inevitable health questions so she could go about her life. And it allowed her oncologist to focus on Sue rather than worry about the right questions to ask.

Bring a Buddy: Having a second set of ears is ideal. It is hard for a patient to take in everything at once.

Exercise: Sue volunteered to be part of the University of Wisconsin Medical School Psychology Department's exercise study involving women with breast cancer. That was a win-win for everyone. Thanks to patients like Sue, we now know that exercise and fitness are essential in prevention and treatment. Sue also felt better physically and emotionally because she knew she was helping other women treat or prevent breast cancer.

Stay Ahead of the Pain: Sue saw others endure the horrific pain of bone cancer, so she asked her oncologist how to stay ahead of the pain with appropriate medicine. In addition, she read about the importance of palliative care and contacted hospice to initiate that relationship.

Advocacy: "I am a beginner at breast cancer advocacy," Sue wrote in a scholarship application to the National Breast Cancer Coalition advocacy training in Washington, DC. Sue noted her involvement in local support groups for metastatic breast cancer patients:

I try to speak up in these groups, let others know what I've read and heard that might be useful to them. I also tell everyone who will listen what happened to me, so that it won't happen to them.

What happened to me was a missed diagnosis; despite getting mammograms for eight years and being sent to a surgeon for a biopsy two years before the diagnosis, I was diagnosed at Stage IV, with metastases to the bones.

If I had been a better advocate for myself, I have no doubt that it would have been caught earlier.

Extending my personal experience out, I think that there are many women who let doctors and HMOs and insurance companies bully them out of good medical care the way that I did. If they were armed with better information than I had, maybe they could learn to shove back.

I know from personal experience with other young women with metastatic disease that there are many of us just trying to hang around long enough for enough research to be done to transform metastatic disease from a 100% fatal disease to a mere chronic condition. We need the research dollars now!

I have a long-standing interest in government, politics, and the decision-making process, and really do feel, as the saying goes, that the personal is political. My missed diagnosis is part of a much larger problem, a problem that will only be solved by drawing a lot more attention and funding to it.

Support: Support is an essential but challenging piece. It is crushing to feel powerless and ask for someone else's help. Sue didn't want to bother anyone but eventually acknowledged that she appreciated being with her pack.

Sue wasn't a big believer in support groups, but she did find value in connecting with other women with breast cancer. They formed a "Green Bananas" group, so named because they planned to be around long enough to eat the bananas after they ripened. She also was part of Bosom Buddies and Instant Sisters, local groups for women with metastatic breast cancer. Theirs was an instant bond.

Helping others was a priority, and Sue helped numerous women in Madison and even a coworker of mine.

Support from family, friends, and her spouse was crucial. We all voraciously researched breast cancer and shared summaries with Sue. The three daughters and Mom joined the thousands of participants in Madison's Race for the Cure. Sue and Kevin had participated the previous year while the rest of us did local runs.

Attendance at Mayo Clinic meetings was another way to support Sue. We learned about the latest research, complementary/alternative therapies, and clinical trials and heard stories of incredible courage. Experts discussed the importance of exercising, eating fruits and vegetables, being an advocate for one's health, and having a solid relationship with one's practitioner. We each attended different breakout sessions, took notes, and reported back to Sue and one another. It provided empowerment and support for us all.

Caring Bridge was in its infancy at that time, but it has grown to be a powerful way to harness technology for online support. It empowers the individual to update concerned family and friends with one website update rather than responding to each individual.

Hope and Purpose: "Hope is helping ourselves push on every day," noted one cancer survivor at a cancer conference.

"When I get up each day, I hope that I will make a positive difference in someone else's day," she said. "I look for the positives in people and in myself. I look for the most joy I can get out of each day. I don't want to waste this day; it's all I have."

Laughter Is the Best Medicine

Continue to take your prescribed medicines. But be sure to have a regular dose of laughter.

I miss Susie every day of the week and especially her sense of humor. Sue loved a good belly laugh, often at herself in a good-natured, self-deprecating way. Much of our laughter was hearty and off the cuff, but some was intentional because we knew what we each enjoyed. So just a few stories to share …

Opera Time: One of Sue's passions was opera. Although we three sisters were exposed to many cultural activities as we grew up, we also were raised not to be hoity-toity. And to me, opera fringed on hoity-toity.

But I wanted to understand what Sue loved about it. We met in Chicago; our first stop was at the Field Museum to see the dead sea scrolls exhibit. Then we headed off to the Art Institute of Chicago. As a map lover and intrepid explorer, Sue quickly got us around the Chicago metropolis. And remember, this was before the advent of satellite-based navigational systems.

Soon it was time for the opera. I wasn't sure what clothing would be appropriate, but I tried my best to fit in. As we entered the beautiful Civic Opera House with its striking art deco interior, I was nervous that I might look like a country bumpkin and embarrass my sister. I quickly skimmed the plot synopsis to gain some clue as to what would transpire on stage. As the curtain opened and the music began, I understood why Sue was intrigued with opera. The stage lights dimmed, and the orchestra gathered steam. They sang of universal, timeless themes—love, courage, fear, and hubris. I saw Sue's face shine with sheer delight.

When we returned to the real world at intermission, I tried to make the right impression on regular opera aficionados. So I presented a knowing smile but not a toothy one. I worked to subdue my enthusiasm as I told Sue how much I'd enjoyed the opera, adding a purposeful nod here and there. Then I glanced downward. Something was odd.

In our rush to get to the opera on time, Sue had put on two different styles of shoes. I think they were a right and a left, each on the proper foot. But they were clearly *very different* shoes. We looked down at her shoes again, then back up at each other's faces, and broke the hushed tones in the lobby with uncontrollable from-the-gut laughter that we could not stop.

Intermission just wasn't long enough.

Just the Fax: We both enjoyed the off-the-wall humor of *The Far Side* cartoons, and I received a daily calendar of them for Christmas. I regularly faxed them to Sue so we could share a virtual chuckle. One of our favorites was a cartoon of dinosaurs hanging out and smoking cigarettes. The caption read: "Why dinosaurs went extinct."

Our son, Christopher, just six years old when Sue was diagnosed with cancer, also provided a goldmine of lighthearted stories, like this one I emailed her: "Thought you would want to hear this Christopher story. At Sunday School, they had a lesson about the 'Boogie Man' (and how God is always with us, so we don't need to fear). Christopher asked me who the Boogie Man was, but before I could answer, he said, 'I think it's Elvis.'"

Junk Food Buffet: "Let's have a movie night and junk food buffet," Sue announced one morning when I was visiting. We shared many profound discussions while also being disciplined about eating healthy foods. It was time to serve up something that was just plain fun. We rented an irreverent, junior high–humor type of comedy movie and laughed our way through a smorgasbord of high-carb, high-salt, no-redeemable-nutrient-value junk food.

Supermarket Tabloids: The weekly tabloids were rich fodder for laughs, so I usually brought one for my visits. "Fat Tourist Wrecks Tower of Pisa," screamed the headline of one of our favorites. "Leaning landmark nearly topples over during visit! Italian authorities to sue." We anxiously looked for the continuation of the story inside. "She was-a too fat!" said the pope, his hands upraised as he exclaimed, "Mama Mia!"

In this blockbuster issue, the other top stories were "Exorcists Battle Demon Toupee" and the latest fashion trend—"Meat Hats," featuring a photo of a man casually wearing a turkey on his head.

Sue, Kevin, and I talked about quitting our day jobs and starting our own tabloid.

Memorials and Funerals: "I do not want anything named in my memory," Sue said in one of our phone conversations. However, someone had recently contributed to a cancer fundraiser in Sue's honor. "It's as though I'm good as dead," she said, acknowledging that they meant well.

I was at a loss for words. I didn't want to think of a time when anyone would do memorials for my sister. But someday in the distant future, someone might like to contribute something to honor her, as we'd done for our grandparents. Like a tree, for example, because Sue loved trees. "What if someone wants to plant a tree in your memory?" I asked. "Only if it's a native," she quickly answered, and then we both had to laugh about the horrific absurdity of what we needed to discuss these days.

As uncomfortable as it made us, Sue wanted to discuss her funeral service. But, of course, she was most interested in ensuring those who attended received a lovely meal. She had a particular caterer in mind and ideas for the menu. "It puts the fun into funerals when you can talk about them ahead of time!" the consummate hostess declared to her stunned family.

Heaven: The three daughters and our mom were sitting in the living room, curled up in blankets, trying to identify birds at the feeders, talking, and feeling grateful for a chance to hang out with one another.

"I'm not afraid to die," Sue suddenly announced. We all sat bolt upright. "I do hope, though, that heaven will be an interesting place, that there will be enough to do there!"

Clear the Clutter

Clear the clutter so that you may be still and know God.

In our society, marketing gurus help convince us that our material possessions or high-roller lifestyle define us. Or, as Sue had done, we let our possessions give us value. Before she passed away, she realized her value was innate.

Park Avenue Clutter

Linda had lived a glamorous, jet-set life in the fast lane, hobnobbing with celebrities and interviewing multimillionaires.

Through hard work and perseverance, my mom's cousin, Linda, had succeeded in the "city that never sleeps." She was smart, beautiful, and talented and worked as a staff writer and editor for prominent fashion publications and jet-set magazines. She lived in an apartment on exclusive Park Avenue, home to some of New York City's most expensive real estate. One of Linda's friends commented that Linda would confidently stride down Park Avenue as though it was hers— "It should be called Linda Avenue," the New York City lawyer said, chuckling.

Linda came back to Clear Lake occasionally to see her mom, and we connected as adults. It was fun to hear about her exciting adventures. She reminded us that she'd learned to waterski in

Clear Lake, which came in handy when she skied with Ferdinand Marcos, president of the Philippines. His security men surrounded them in boats; some even wore scuba diving gear. Marcos soon fell. Linda didn't want to upstage the president, so she considered dropping as well, but she was more concerned about the sharks and reluctantly hung on. The interview went well anyway.

We spent time with her while on a trip to New York City. She took us to the famed Four Seasons restaurant and later to the private club where celebrities hung out. Linda embodied New York, New York.

But somewhere along the way, the supposed glamor of her life sadly began to unravel. Her photographer partner sold all the celebrity photos taken during their joint interviews to a major photography house but didn't share the profits with Linda. In addition, Linda was getting older in a city where young, glamorous trophy wives were prized.

And then Linda developed ovarian cancer. She had to quit her full-time job and instead worked from home as the Park Avenue Astrologer, doing horoscopes for celebrities.

I took a day off work to attend Linda's mom's funeral, which was held ninety miles away. Linda was pleased and surprised that I had taken the time to do that. "We are family," I replied. "That's what family does."

Her health took a turn for the worse, and she was hospitalized at Sloan-Kettering Hospital. Linda had divorced after a brief marriage and had no relatives nearby. She asked if we would come to NYC to help take care of her apartment and other matters.

We brought her the special foods she craved from the nearby grocery store and helped get the nurse's attention to treat her pain. We talked about the many famous people she interviewed. Later, a friend stopped by to say hello, and we all had a chance to converse. He grew up living in Bermuda and reached a career pinnacle as an interior decorator in "The City That Never Sleeps."

So the two friends could have some time together, we left

to pick up some things from her apartment in the Trump Park Avenue building. When we returned, Linda was gazing from her hospital bed toward the Hudson River. "I have had a fun life!" she said. "I wouldn't change a thing." Later, when Tom left the room, she warned me about the fickleness of men. She noted that young women are the ones in the spotlight, while older women are relegated to the shadows in New York City.

A few days later, we had to head back home. "We love you," I said with a final hug. "God and angels watch over you."

"I love you," was her whispered reply, her eyes heavy with approaching sleep. Linda Ashland, an orphan who was adopted in infancy and grew up to become famous in the Big Apple, passed away about a month later at age sixty-seven.

Linda, too, had been trying to clear the clutter of life in those final months. While sorting through her apartment, I found a draft manuscript she had told me she was writing about an insider's view of high society. Linda noted that her experience "provided me with unique background material about the world of high fashion, society, and politics ... I have particular insight into the struggles for status. The schemes, conniving and intrigues undertaken by people to appear in these publications and the preying upon of editors and reporters of these magazines who often suffer the very same weaknesses and ambitions.

"In many ways, what these people say and do affects all of our lives by creating and setting certain standards. These standards, whether real or artificial, often become the criteria that determine 'the fashion' and success or failure in a multi-million-dollar business world ..."

Her closets were full of gowns and shoes from an earlier heyday. A sign in her front doorway referenced women's need for courage and wit in their struggle for equality and long life.

As a young woman, Linda had been anxious to leave her hometown and experience the bright city lights. Yet, she'd saved years of her class reunion information, numerous letters from her mom and dad, Christmas cards, and other personal correspondence. They were stacked on her desk by the music box that played "Somewhere Over the Rainbow."

Slow Down—Today Is a Gift

Pundits like to call this the "Golden Age of Anxiety."

It is a world where multitasking and being over-the-top busy is a virtue; twenty-four-hour news always has the latest breaking crisis, and twenty-four-hour social media is always beckoning.

Research has started to quantify what we already know in our gut—that we are affected when TV news shows us child victims of chemical warfare, school shootings, or natural disasters. It does not matter that these realities are half a world away. They can still make us feel sad and anxious.

I was walking from work to my car in the parking lot when I noticed a young mom. She looked harried as she bustled across the street with her toddler in tow. "Hurry up," she said and tossed a bag into the front seat as her child scrambled into the van. Then she started backing the van out and almost rammed another car in the parking lot.

I watched as the vehicle sped out of the parking lot. The van had a vanity license plate—IMINAHURRY.

Rather than cramming just one more thing on our to-do list, we can take the time to be present and focus on the people and activities around us. For example, a pastor told a story at a recent funeral about a friend who spent several hours sharing treasured memories with his aging father at the nursing home. As mealtime neared, the friend gave his father a hearty hug and drove away toward home. But within just minutes, his cell phone rang. His father had just collapsed and died.

"Remember that life can change in the blink of an eye," the pastor said. So be thankful for each day and one another.

Focus on the Positive

I often asked my gram, "How do you do this?" How did she stay positive, calm, and respectful of others? Life can have such challenges; some people can be such a challenge. She told me always to try to put myself in the other person's shoes and to see situations from their perspective. Acknowledge that everyone faces battles at different stages in their life. As a Christian who exemplified her faith, gentleness, kindness, and goodness seemed to be second nature to her.

She also said to pray—*often!*

Gram suggested that I read a book called *The Power of Positive Thinking* by Dr. Norman Vincent Peale. But I was a know-it-all college kid by this time, so I poopooed it as old-fashioned and irrelevant.

Because of my "I'm too cool for that old-time stuff" arrogance, I missed the opportunity to discuss this important concept with my gram. After she passed away, I found her copy of the book. By reading the introduction, I learned that the author wanted to find a way to resolve the pain of his boyhood feelings of inferiority and shyness. He wrote that we don't need to be defeated by anything and that our lives can be full of satisfaction and joy. *Come on, that is just being naïve.* But I read on despite my skepticism. The concept of the power of positive thinking doesn't ignore or sugarcoat life's problems but provides a practical system based on spiritual techniques. So I got out my highlighter and read on.

> Finally, brothers and sisters, whatever is true,
> whatever is noble, whatever is right, whatever is
> pure, whatever is lovely, whatever is admirable—
> if anything is excellent or praiseworthy—think
> about such things. (Philippians 4:8 NIV)

Let's Ramp It Up

The previous "Reconnection" section laid out a solid foundation of steps to become that better, not bitter, version of oneself after facing one of life's storms. Sharing your lessons learned with someone going through the same storm, best practices for someone with a life-threatening medical issue, and remembering to value ourselves and one another, not our material possessions, are just some of the initial steps of our My Better Self plan. Let's take time to focus on one another, not on our to-do lists.

That is a great start. But like any workout or physical fitness plan, sometimes we start with good intentions and then hit the doldrums. I don't know about you, but I tend to self-congratulate if I make even the tiniest progress in any physical fitness plan I start. Exercising for even fifteen minutes a week is much better than just thinking about it, right? Unfortunately, I also fall into a habit of occasionally thinking, *Well, I haven't changed that much since college.* So that is when I need the stand-in-front-of-the-mirror shock treatment.

Yikes! Or, as Sue would say, "Take a bite of the Reality Burger."

This pithy reminder helps me face some hard facts—there have been a few changes since college all those years ago. That is why another choice should be to …

Wake Up!

My two sisters, our dog, our cat, and I would all be jolted from our sweet slumber with a *Bzzzzzt, zzzzttt, phhhht—Time to wake up! Now!"*

Our mom's voice over the scratchy intercom system, punctuated by elevator music and hog futures, was a startling but effective way to get three teenagers on their way, clambering to be the first in the shower.

And there was another subtle Mom admonition in our family: whenever we three girls would say we couldn't find something, our mom would reply, "Just open your eyes!"

Sue's breast cancer trumped Mom's shouts as a raw wake-up call to life. In her final days, Sue said she would have done the following:

Loved more.

Forgiven more.

Been closer to her family.

There is no dress rehearsal. Life is what happens while you're making plans. It's time to open our eyes.

Take out the Garbage

Let's start by taking out the garbage.

Excuse me?

Picture an enormous garbage can.

We figuratively pitch all kinds of things in there throughout our lives. Disappointments, tragedies, other people's disparaging comments toward us, a lack of self-confidence, childhood experiences, regrets, mistreatments, poor decisions, misdirected anger, and the list unfurls of what we want to discard. But it starts to pile up if we keep stuffing all of this away without paying attention. And then it starts to stink. And then it gets so cumbersome that it becomes immovable.

Instead of mindlessly chucking our experiences in there, hoping that someone else will clean them out for us, we need to sort through them to see what barriers keep us from growing into our better selves. Some are probably worth examining more closely to learn a nugget instead of just repeating. Or they're valuable in ensuring we won't hurt others the same way. Finally, there may be some that we can reframe or recycle in a different direction for life.

Perhaps a professional counselor is needed to help us sort through our garbage cans. Self-help groups or books can be a resource. It's a worthwhile journey to ensure that we are not just repeating family tragedies. But no matter the quality or quantity of our garbage, we all must acknowledge its existence. No city garbage crew is going to haul this can away. It is our garbage.

Likewise, humankind has a collective garbage can. *Phew!* This one stinks even more. Many of us, or our ancestors in the generations before us, have contributed to it. But likewise, we need to face the fact that it exists. Then we can take action to help ensure a better world.

Here are just some of the more recent and pungent items in our collective garbage:

Loneliness

We may have more people than ever on this planet, but we are lonely. We have the technology to stay in touch twenty-four hours a day and countless friends on Facebook, but pundits dubbed us the loneliest generation ever.

According to census figures and research, about eight million people in the US, or about one in eleven Americans aged fifty and older, do not have a spouse, partner, or living child. That means baby boomers are aging alone more than any generation in US history.

In England, the British government appointed a minister for loneliness after research determined that nine million people in the United Kingdom often or always feel lonely.

Mental Health

Research shows that an unprecedented number of high school and middle school students are experiencing mental health problems, due at least in part to social media pressures and exacerbated by the coronavirus.

Suicides were up in all age groups in the US in the past decade, but the increase in teenage and young adult suicides outpaced the other groups. The phrase "deaths of despair" was coined to explain the disturbing and dramatically rising trend over the past few decades of white, blue-collar deaths from suicide, drug and opioid overdoses, and alcoholism.

Both trends contributed to the longest overall downward trend in life expectancy in the United States since 1918. Centers for Disease Control officials said those sobering statistics should be a wake-up call that the country is losing too many Americans to preventable conditions.

Climate Change

For the past several years, we have seen record floods, droughts, wildfires, hurricanes, and extreme heat, which have displaced millions of people worldwide.

The past decade was the hottest ever recorded on the planet. As a result, some US oceanside military bases are in danger of collapsing into a rising ocean. A warming sea turbocharged Hurricane Ian to create a monster storm surge, trapping thousands of Floridians in their homes, killing over one hundred, and destroying communities. Nearly one-fifth of some of our planet's oldest living organisms, the giant sequoia trees in California, have been destroyed in mega-wildfires. In Pakistan, massive floods killed over one thousand people, displaced millions, and wiped out food supplies. According to a United Nations report, one million plant and animal species are on the verge of extinction.

Why should we care about these unfathomable numbers? Because they have alarming implications for each of us—our very survival, the impact on our economy, livelihoods, food security and supply, and quality of life worldwide. In addition, because the federal government often acts as an insurer of last resort in helping communities, families, and businesses recover from extreme weather events, the growing billions of dollars in damages will add new pressures on government budgets and taxpayers.

The Paris Agreement in 2015 provided hope to address this global emergency to reduce greenhouse gas emissions. With an international review every five years, leaders in many countries worldwide looked to 2020 as the year to launch initiatives. But the global pandemic took center stage instead. Experts say we are at a climate crossroads. In 2021, the United Nations secretary-general described it as a "code red for humanity." In 2022, he said the world is heading into "uncharted territories of destruction."

A much-anticipated report in 2023 provided a glimmer of hope and a sense of urgency. "A liveable future for all is possible if we take urgent climate action," according to the Intergovernmental Panel on Climate Change United Nations report. This report was based on years of work by hundreds of scientists worldwide. "Time is short, but there is a clear path forward."

Technology developed in recent years needs to be fast-tracked and made available worldwide. Governments are vital to making this happen through public funding, clear signals to investors, and "tried and tested" policy measures. However, it will take massive investment and global cooperation. "Transformational changes are more likely to succeed where there is trust, where everyone works together to prioritize risk reduction, and where benefits and burdens are shared equitably," said IPCC Chair Hoesung Lee.

Mistrust and Misinformation

Frustration about our elected leaders' polarization, the relentless spewing of public vitriol, and countless sources of misinformation create an environment ripe for mistrust, according to national polls. In addition, credible and reliable news sources have become minimized because other organizations focus on the public's appetite for TV's quick sound bites and entertainment. While print news sources are disappearing, options for TV news have exploded, meaning more networks are competing for eyeballs and reaching out to niche audiences for their twenty-four-hour coverage.

Polls show that about half of American adults get news from social media, even though tech companies have come under heavy scrutiny for allowing misinformation to spread across their platforms.

Even cybersecurity rules add to distrust, alerting us to be hyperalert when we use our devices online at work and even from our homes, for fear of being duped by a malicious hacker.

Hate Groups and Crimes

Hate groups burst into our living rooms as we had front-row seats to the TV news and stark images of unmasked neo-Nazis in the "Unite the Right" rally in 2017 in Charlottesville, Virginia. Several marchers carried torches, wore swastikas, and shouted, "Jews will not replace us" to the television cameras. The protest turned violent as the driver of a car plowed into a crowd, killing one and injuring many.

The deadliest attack on the Jewish community in United States history occurred in October 2018, when a gunman opened fire at the Tree of Life synagogue in Pittsburgh, Pennsylvania. Shabbat morning services were being held when a man armed with an AR-15 rifle and pistols entered and killed eleven congregants and wounded seven. He had posted anti-Semitic slurs online just before the shooting.

In Christchurch, New Zealand, a self-described white nationalist live streamed his slaughter of fifty people worshipping in two mosques on Facebook. He purportedly wrote a manifesto about seeking revenge and copycatting a massacre in Norway. He intentionally chose remote and placid New Zealand to show that no place on earth was safe.

In 2022, an eighteen-year-old white male researched areas with large concentrations of Black people and then went on a shooting rampage at a Buffalo, New York, supermarket. He broadcast his rampage live online. Ten people were murdered, and others were injured while grocery shopping.

Just ten days after the rampage in Buffalo, an eighteen-year-old killed nineteen young children and two adults at an elementary school in Uvalde, Texas. Mass killings in the US were already at a record pace for the year and occurring in grocery stores, theaters, shopping malls, churches, schools, and other public spaces.

Experts note that groups have used the internet to help spawn the radicalization of "lone wolf" terrorists. In addition, social media and uninhibited political rhetoric have fueled the rise of public expressions of hatred of different groups and its "normalization" for younger generations.

Racism

Even though the subjugation of other races is a story as old as civilization, we can't classify it as ancient history.

While visiting Cape Town, South Africa, an elderly gentleman told us how his family and neighbors still suffer financial and educational damage from the government's abolished policy of apartheid. Tears rolled down his cheeks as he explained how the government suddenly forced his family and all others in the thriving District 6 neighborhood to leave their homes in the city proper and move to a barren, outlying area. The government bulldozed their homes, and construction soon began on new homes for an all-white district.

In Peru, we saw how indigenous people who moved from rural areas to the cities for jobs live in shanty towns on the edges of Lima. In northern Manitoba, Canada, a Sayisi Dene woman explained how the Canadian government forcibly airlifted them away from their nomadic caribou hunting grounds and into the town of Churchill in 1956. With no way to continue their livelihoods, half of their population was dead within two decades.

And in Myanmar, Syria, Yemen, South Sudan, Central Africa, and on and on across the globe, we read about ongoing racial and religious conflict. It is so heartbreaking and overwhelming that sometimes we need to tune it out.

But sadness, horror, and outrage erupted worldwide when we saw a video of a Minneapolis, Minnesota, police officer jamming his knee on the neck of an unarmed, handcuffed Black man until he died.

George Floyd was arrested for allegedly using a counterfeit twenty-dollar bill at a local store. Other officers stood by as George Floyd pleaded with the officer to get his knee off his neck because he could not breathe. He cried out for his mother, and shortly after, this son, husband, and father died.

A bystander's video went viral.

Thousands of protestors streamed into Minneapolis streets. What began as peaceful demonstrations later spiraled into looting and burning of buildings—even the police precinct station—as darkness set in. Local leaders called for calm and demanded accountability while supporting demonstrators' constitutional right to protest peacefully.

More protests soon erupted nationwide and worldwide, reigniting the Black Lives Matter movement. "Why does my being born Black mean I will never be equal?" one of the Black Lives Matter protestors asked a news reporter.

PART III

Build the Muscle

Muster the Courage to Act

Okay. That was depressing. These facts are brutal to face. I have enough of my own garbage without even considering our collective garbage. So maybe I'll throw up my hands in defeat and hope I won't crumble when faced with life's next challenge.

Or, I instead could remember that challenges and storms are inevitable for individuals and societies. Then I could recall the stories of inspirational people like Mary, Craig, Hedi, Mary Ann, Char, and Sue, who chose to face their daunting challenges and become better, not bitter. Their examples helped make the world a better place.

The first step forward is to consider if there are personal barriers that some of us need to address before forging ahead. Perhaps a judgmental comment like "Just who do you think you are, trying to do that?" handcuffed you in the past. Or you remember what it felt like when other kids laughed at you for saying you wanted to try something different. Perhaps you were punished for trying to better yourself. Fear of the unknown is a common reaction. Even today, when I step outside of my comfort zone, I can almost hear myself say, "But I'm too little." That was my go-to phrase when my older sisters and their friends tried to goad me into some new (often suspect) activity.

"We are taught to understand, correctly, that courage is not the absence of fear but the capacity for action despite our fears," the late Senator John McCain and former prisoner of war wrote in his book *Why Courage Matters* (John McCain and Marshall Salter, Random House, 2004).

"I've been absolutely terrified every moment of my life, and I've never let it keep me from doing a single thing that I wanted to do," said famed American painter Georgia O'Keefe. Her bold, abstract watercolors helped pave the way for American modernism.

We can take comfort in knowing that generations before us had similar fears.

> I alone cannot change the world, but I can cast a stone across the waters to create many ripples. (Mother Teresa, *A Simple Path*, Ballantine Books, October 31, 1995)

My Better Self: Pivotal Steps

After identifying our obstacles and with other generations urging us forward, let's take action to keep growing with the next phase of My Better Self.

With most physical workout plans, individuals focus on the key activities that will be most impactful. Likewise, here are some pivotal steps to include in your My Better Self plan to get through life's storms with grace.

Take an Attitude Check

"The greatest discovery of my generation is that a human being can alter his life by altering his attitude" (William James, leading nineteenth-century American philosopher and psychologist).

"Our minds are a special gift from God," Pastor Harlan said, noting the mind can store more than one hundred trillion thoughts. "We need to choose what we think about. What we put in our minds affects the way we act. As Paul said in Philippians 4:8, '... whatever is true, whatever is noble, whatever is right, whatever is pure, whatever is lovely, whatever is admirable—if anything is excellent or praiseworthy, think about such things.'"

Cultivate an Attitude of Gratitude

Researchers tell us what our gut already knows: an attitude of gratitude is one of the healthiest things we can do for ourselves.

But gratitude is not necessarily in our nature. On the contrary, it seems we humans have an insatiable appetite for more, no matter how much we already have. It is not a new trait. Even after being freed from slavery in Egypt, the Israelites grumbled about not having enough food and, next, about not having the right kind of food. Contemporary marketers focus on this with their taglines of *more* speed, *more* food, and *more* possessions.

I thought back to our family's first Thanksgiving together after Sue's cancer diagnosis. Sue had always loved Thanksgiving because of its focus on pure and straightforward thankfulness for life's gifts. She sent me a note telling me she just wanted to focus on being thankful for being together and not dwell on the cancer news. It was Sue who led the prayer at the dinner table. We joined hands to say thanks for many blessings: being together, having food to eat, homes to live in, and the gift of life.

Sue shared her gratefulness for the rest of her life—candy for the nurses who did her IVs, special meals for caregivers, and gifts for her pets' veterinarians to show her appreciation for their care. Sue did this because she felt it was important to do, and it also gave her joy. Recent scientific studies have revealed that a grateful attitude also can provide health benefits. For example, grateful people have fewer aches and pains; gratitude improves mental health; it helps people feel more empathetic and less likely to seek revenge; it can enhance self-esteem and foster resilience. In addition, an earlier study found that gratitude significantly contributed to stability after the 9/11 terror attacks.

A family friend, Edith, was one of those who inspired us with her enduring attitude of gratitude. Her firstborn, Ralph, developed cerebral palsy, but she forged ahead with her indomitable spirit and thankfulness. Her second son, Robert, became a famous cardiac surgeon. Because state institutions could not meet Ralph's adult needs, Edith and Robert helped create an organization that became a nationwide model for caring for adults with disabilities.

Edith, in her late eighties, spoke at a Thanksgiving service at our church. "Thanksgiving is not so much counting our blessings as making our blessings count," she said. "So at Thanksgiving, consider making it an everyday way of life. God's gifts to us are not solely ours, but rather we are to use these gifts throughout our lives to help others."

How do we cultivate a grateful attitude despite life's inevitable difficulties?

We can gratefully remember that everything has come from God and belongs to God, Pastor Harlan noted. We can be grateful for the grace He has shown us in that He forgives, heals, and is slow to anger. Finally, we can be thankful that God has a plan for us.

Pastor Harlan suggested that when you wake up each day, sit on the edge of your bed and thank God for five to ten things. Continue that conversation of thankfulness throughout the day and wrap up each day by stating your gratefulness. Thank God no matter what happens—not *for* the circumstance but *in* the circumstance because God remains faithful through it all. "When we are grateful, it gets the focus off our problems and gets the focus on the benefits in our lives," he said. "Develop the attitude of gratitude and watch your stress level go down."

Rather than taking things for granted, be thankful for a roof over your head and food in the refrigerator. Instead of fretting about buying just the right present for someone, *be* present.

The more grateful we are, the less we compare, and the easier it is to see when someone else is hurting rather than to stand in judgment.

Mary, the mother of the teenage girl who committed suicide, knew she needed to be very intentional about focusing on thankfulness, or she would be consumed in a tailspin of grief and regrets. So she disciplined herself to write a list of the many things she was grateful for each day.

Create Patches of Green

That courageous, thankful attitude makes it easier to create "patches of green" in what can seem a parched world.

I loved seeing the snowcapped Mount St. Helens as one of a trio of mountain peaks visible from the Lewis and Clark College campus in nearby Portland. What a marvelous view for future generations to enjoy. But part of that scenic view suddenly disappeared in 1980 with the most destructive volcanic eruption in US history, killing fifty-seven people and thousands of animals and destroying over two hundred homes.

"The intense heat melted the soil and left bare rock coated with a thick mantle of ash," Phillip Yancy wrote in his book *What's So Amazing About Grace* (Zondervan, 1997). "Forest Service naturalists wondered how much time must pass before any living thing could grow there. One day, a naturalist noticed an area of grasses, wildflowers, and ferns sprouting amid the desolation. On closer examination, he saw that it formed the shape of an elk that the ash had buried. Properly seeded …" these patches of green brought new life to "…the otherwise barren landscape."

Yancy compared those patches of green to what happened in the nineteenth century when Victorian England was scarred by slavery in the colonies, child labor in factories, and squalor in the cities. He posited that after a society begins to decay, signs of its former life, the ingrained "habits of the heart," reassert themselves. Like the regenerating vegetation on Mount St. Helens, the change came from below. Ordinary British citizens listened to their hearts and formed nearly five hundred charitable volunteer organizations to address these needs.

Spread Kindness

Likewise, after the horrific massacre of twenty youngsters and six teachers by a shooter at Sandy Hook Elementary School in Connecticut, an educator wanted to rekindle hope with what became Secret Kindness Agents.

Omaha, Nebraska, teacher Ferial Pearson asked her high school students if a modest act of compassion could change the course of a life. Students compiled a list of ten to fifteen potential benefits and risks, then brainstormed possible acts of kindness they could perform anonymously. The anonymity helped generate selflessness and empathy as students shared positive actions throughout the community.

"It helped the students become more sensitive to the needs of others," Pearson explained in an article. "It helps them to see beyond themselves and changes their view of the world."

Teachers and students have replicated this model at schools around the country.

Be a Barnabas

Think back to a time when someone listened to you with compassion rather than judgment or criticism. That person's caring and encouraging spirit helped you to move forward instead of wallowing in what-ifs.

In a time of constant social media mudslinging and so many clamoring to be center stage, aspire instead to be a Barnabas. More than two thousand years ago, Joseph, a native of Cyprus, sold a field he owned and put the money he received at the feet of the apostles. He was "a good man, full of the Holy Spirit and faith" (Acts 11:24 NIV). He was nicknamed Barnabas or "son of encouragement" for his many acts of faith in the early Christian church.

Apostle Paul speaks to us today as he did to his fellow missionaries:

> Therefore, encourage one another and build each
> other up. (1Thessalonians 5:11 NIV)

Ditch the Labels

Except when she lost her hair for a time, strangers couldn't tell that Sue had a life-threatening disease. So I sometimes found myself frustrated if someone barged in line or scooted into a parking space before Sue could. "Don't you know that my sister has *cancer*?" I wanted to shout. But, of course, they didn't know.

Instead of overreacting, it is good to remember that we don't know what battles others are fighting. Treating others as we wish to be treated is a tenet taught to us by our parents and religions worldwide.

Research shows that respectful people are the happiest. These aren't doormat-nice people, nor so "nice" that they don't tell a doctor they are wrong in their diagnosis. Instead, these people are the version of nice that includes mutual kindness and respect. They take the time to ponder a kind response in a disagreement instead of a knee-jerk emotional rant. This issue isn't new to our human race. Check out this scripture regarding how to treat one another in approximately AD 60:

> My dear brothers and sisters, take note of this:
> Everyone should be quick to listen, slow to speak
> and slow to become angry. (James 1:19 NIV)

Being respectful also means not labeling others. Labels mean we don't have to take time to talk with someone, hear their story, and get to know them as individuals. Instead, we can dismiss them as a (insert label here). Done.

But aren't we each much more complicated and interesting than the clothes we wear, the car we drive, or our hairstyle? "Don't put me in a box," said a friend who is both a pastor and a lawyer. We were not designed to be carbon copies of one another. Instead, we each have our personalized DNA, our unique fingerprints. Even the natural world has diversity and uniqueness—zebras each have distinctive stripes, wolves their unique howls, and each snowflake is one of a kind.

Dig Deeper

Even those who intentionally try to avoid labeling need to consider digging deeper. Like a snake sliding its way into a campground, prejudice and bias may slither unnoticed into our lives.

I was sorting through some old books that had been stored away and noticed my grandmother's grammar school geography book, published in 1902. I thought it would be interesting to see if our concepts have changed.

I turned to a section called "Races of Men." I was astonished to read some of the following descriptions: Blacks in Africa south of the Sahara: "Such natives are very ignorant ... Such people are savages"; the "red race" (Amazon tribes) "hunt and fish, and lead a lazy, shiftless life"; the "yellow race" (Japanese) have been "wise enough to adopt many of the customs of the white man." Last but not least, "the white race" is "now the leading race in the world." Whoa! Surely my grandparents hadn't believed this in their young lives. They certainly did not as adults.

Social scientists are telling us today that even if we don't have a ranting, name-calling side to us, each of us has unconscious biases, whether it is regarding race, gender, religion, or even someone's hairstyle. In the book *Blindspot: Hidden Biases of Good People* (Mahzarin Banaji and Greenwald, Anthony G. Bantam, 2016), the authors describe how we are just now learning that our life experiences unconsciously impact our assessments of others. Weight and age can also play into our judgments. For example, do you ever notice an overweight person and think, *Why don't they do something about that?* Or do you ever see an older adult shuffling along and say to yourself, *Why can't they just hurry it up?* Or do you have a preconception that someone who lives in New York is pushy and someone in the Midwest is an uneducated bumpkin?

If we don't self-examine, our actions can cause pain and suffering to those around us.

Truly Listen and Learn

Sadly, it may take an extreme example, like the horrific death of George Floyd, to wake us up.

At last, we might finally hear our neighbors' painful stories of daily life. One Black man told a reporter that he needed his daughters to accompany him on walks around his Minneapolis suburban neighborhood so the neighbors wouldn't call the police about a "suspicious" Black man. Other Black fathers said they are tired of seeing surprised expressions and snickers when they talk about how much they enjoy spending time with their kids.

Shake Your Family Tree

It is also helpful for each of us to shake our family trees. Most likely, at least some of our branches include immigrants. Yet some of us celebrate it, some hide it, and some are clueless about our heritage.

We have vacillated between welcoming and shunning immigrants throughout our nation's history. Immigrants with a European background tended to be most welcome, especially when we needed more worker bees.

I witnessed some of this history. After the US withdrew from Vietnam, Indochinese allies of the United States were left to face imprisonment, torture, and death by the ruling communist regime. Iowa's Governor Robert Ray was the only governor in the nation to respond to President Gerald Ford's appeal to help resettle Southeast Asians after the war. "I didn't think we could just sit here idly and say, 'Let those people die,'" Ray said in an Iowa public TV documentary.

Not all Iowans agreed, as some argued that the immigrants would take jobs from the residents. The governor's response? His aides tallied daily "Help Wanted" ads so the governor could personally inform those critics about current job openings for them to pursue.

When some members of the national governing board of the governor's church voiced concerns about involvement in a politically sensitive issue, Ray went to the church's national convention. "Don't tell me of your concerns for human rights; show me," Ray said. "Don't tell me of your concerns for these people when you have a chance to save their lives; show me. Don't tell me how Christian you are. Show me." The church association became a significant supporter. A statewide fundraising campaign, Iowa SHARES, was successful in helping provide doctors, nurses, food, and supplies for the refugees. Ray reported to Congress that the Tai Dam became productive members of society, paying taxes and earning their way.

If we were all meant to look and act alike, why are we each unique with our individual fingerprints and DNA? Consider the incredible diversity in the natural world—scientists estimate there are over 8.7 million species, with the majority not yet identified.

Take Action to Change the Climate

Not only can we do better with our social climate, but another pivotal step in our Better Self Plan is to help change our physical climate.

Scientists worldwide tell us that our shared home – the

earth – urgently needs help. Compare this to a building inspector determining that our family's house foundation is crumbling. We would prioritize fixing it immediately. Likewise, our international "family" needs to agree on how to get the repair job done for the well-being of our families and future generations.

As the decades of warnings from leaders of the global scientific community and the United Nations became starker, the UN Paris Climate Summit of 2015 provided some hope. That same year, "every living person on this planet" received a spiritual framework with the first-ever papal encyclical written by Pope Francis in "Laudato Si'": "On Care for Our Common Home." He issued a powerful appeal for people to face one of the principal challenges confronting humanity today, to recognize the need for lifestyle, production, and consumption changes and respond to "the cry of the earth and the cry of the poor."

Years later, climate change has become a real-life experience in our backyards and across the globe.

The bottom line is if we don't take meaningful action, we will have to focus on bare-knuckled survival instead of becoming the better people we can be.

Share Your Financial Resources

If the adage "we are blessed so we can be a blessing to others" resonates, there are countless organizations we can uplift worldwide.

Over a decade ago, my husband and I and our fourteen-year-old son got to host two cheerful young boys who were part of the African Children's Choir performing in our hometown. As a result, my mom, husband, and I decided to become educational sponsors. Our first letter from our young sponsor was addressed to "Uncle and Auntie" and was brimful with gratitude and excitement about the tour. In the heartfelt letters we've received throughout the years, we've read about our sponsored child's aspirations as a boy and his life as he grows into a college student. When we hear about civil strife in Kenya, we pray for his safety. He sent his best wishes for the birth of our granddaughter and his hope that she grows to be a strong woman.

How can it get much better than that? As their Music for Life tagline says, "Helping Africa's most vulnerable children today so that they can help Africa tomorrow."

Millions of people have been displaced worldwide in recent years. More than half of the world's forcibly displaced people are children whose families are driven from their homes by war, political oppression, drought, floods, and religious persecution. While it is daunting, financial contributions to agencies such as USA for UNHCR, the UN Refugee Agency, CARE, the Carter Center, and many other programs make a difference. They are committed to helping people rebuild their lives by meeting the basic needs of food, shelter, and medicine with a goal of sustainability.

And in our backyard, numerous nonprofit organizations help meet the needs of many in the United States. Check them out on charity watchdog groups such as Charity Navigator and GuideStar to confirm the percentage of funds used directly to assist people rather than administrative overhead.

Travel to Learn

"A mind that is stretched by a new experience can never go back to its old dimensions," said former Supreme Court Justice Oliver Wendell Holmes Jr.

To some, a new experience might mean a trip to check off the bucket list. But it can be so much more. New experiences can help us understand diversity and our common threads on this planet. Experiencing different geographies provides a context for other cultures. Local guides help ensure that we hear residents' perspectives. Travel is a chance to look into one another's eyes, shake hands, and share stories. And it can lead to that glorious "Ah-ha!" moment of understanding that we all gaze upon the same moon, relish sunsets and sunrises, and have similar challenges as we strive for healthy, productive lives for our families.

President Dwight Eisenhower understood this. He saw firsthand the devastation of war but believed that ordinary citizens wanted peace even if their leaders did not. So, in 1956, he created the People-to-People program so ordinary people could travel and act as ambassadors of peace between countries.

The American Field Service and other student groups were founded on the same premises. The Peace Corps, founded in 1961, was conceived to promote mutual understanding between different people but also to provide social and economic development through technical assistance.

Travel can bring significant chapters in human history to life.

We toured the Kahal Kadosh Shalom (Holy Congregation of Peace)in Rhodes, Greece, the oldest Jewish synagogue in Greece, dating back to the second century BC. The museum next to it depicts the Jewish community's roller-coaster existence of sanctuary and persecution. "We must remember the harm we are capable of doing to others," our museum guide said, "to ensure we do not repeat it."

Our travel group silently stood as we heard the World War II story of how Jewish community leaders were hopeful the Greek island of Rhodes would be spared from Nazi displacement. But on July 18, 1944, a German officer told the president of the Jewish community that all Jewish males over the age of sixteen had to gather the following day with their work permits and identity cards. The Nazis took those documents at the meeting and demanded that the women join their husbands within twenty-four hours, or Nazis would shoot the husbands. In addition, they were to bring their belongings, including jewelry, gold sovereigns, bank notes, and food.

Within just days, the Nazis forced 1,673 men, women, and children through the Rhodes streets. Like cattle, they were herded onto cargo boats and eventually sent to Auschwitz, Poland. The twelve hundred people judged too weak to work were murdered in the gas chambers. Only one hundred fifty survived.

Our guide had told us we could meet a man who survived the Auschwitz Nazi concentration camp and now spends most days at the synagogue sharing his story. Unfortunately, he didn't arrive before the tour ended, but we waited around. Soon, a tall man wearing a yarmulke appeared, looking frustrated. The museum guide explained that the man was sad for missing the tour group, so I asked if the interpreter would help him tell us his story. The guide told us that the man grew up in Italy. But with the onset of World War II, he and his Jewish family were forced to leave their homes and possessions and travel by train to the Auschwitz extermination camp in Germany. The young boy was separated there from his entire family. He never saw them again.

The lone survivor of his family, he became a refugee in postwar Europe. He later moved to Rhodes as an adult. Now in retirement, this was his job. He would tell and retell the story so such tragedies would never again happen.

"I can't begin to tell you how sorry I am for what you have had to endure," I said, looking directly into his dark brown eyes. "Thank you for telling your important story."

We didn't need an interpreter for that. He gave me a big hug.

Get out of Our Echo Chambers and Start a Civil Conversation

Helloooooo in there!

Because we can now customize what news we ingest, it's easy to reinforce our existing beliefs instead of fully informing ourselves using different sources. With this tunnel vision, the world perspective can narrow to us versus them with no room for civil dialogue.

The twenty-four-hour news channels rarely send reporters to get first-person interviews from experts at the scene but instead fill their airtime with opinions. Politicians focus on the six-second sound bite for TV instead of talking in depth with editorial boards. Social media has become the modern-day Colosseum, where instead of gladiators, "Twitter mobs" can take someone down. As a result, rants have become acceptable on the airwaves, in our living rooms, and at our dinner tables.

Instead of a knee-jerk rant or jumping into a Twitter mob, can we all first pause and search for facts on important issues? Next, make it your practice to check out other credible news sources besides social media. Then, in the best interest of our families, communities, and democracies, take a breath, count to ten, and practice the art of respectful conversations. We were told about this centuries ago:

> But the fruit of the Spirit is love, joy, peace, forbearance, kindness, goodness, faithfulness, gentleness, and self-control. Against such things there is no law. (Galatians 5:22–23 NIV)

The world is changed by your example, not your opinion.
—Action for Happiness

Foster Community

One of the plusses of living in a small community like ours is that it offers the opportunity to bring out the best in folks when there is a need. For those living in large cities, a traffic accident may mean the frustrating inconvenience of jamming up rush hour traffic. In a small town, though, the sound of a siren means someone's loved one or friend could be hurt.

Rex McChesney was an affable high school and community college athlete who had worked his way up in law enforcement to be appointed interim police chief. Personally, he was known as a family man and school booster. Professionally, he was known for his respectful treatment of everyone, regardless of stature in life, race, or other issues. In a time when there were widespread racial brutality protests again law enforcement, he set a high bar of mutual respect and fairness.

But then he was diagnosed with pancreatic cancer. A palatable shockwave reverberated through the community. Countless Clear Lake residents tried to figure out how best to support our police chief and his family. A community fundraiser at the new fire department building was a way to proclaim that support.

Posters, Facebook posts, and church bulletin announcements could be seen everywhere in the weeks leading up to the event. The entire community seemed to pass through the fire department doors as people swarmed to hug Rex or shake his hand. Several children wore their T-Rex "Take a bite out of cancer" T-shirts. "I rested all day yesterday just so I could be here today," commented one of the attendees who sat in her wheelchair. She wore a pretty head scarf to cover evidence of her chemo treatments.

Chief McChesney ultimately passed away from cancer. But his memory and the community that rallied behind him will never forget his inspiring spirit.

Share Your Time and Talents

Make a Difference for Children in Your Neighborhood

He wasn't looking to volunteer for another nonprofit organization that could benefit from his attorney skills.

But he agreed to join the board of Greater Iowa Youth for Christ and soon saw that it had a "charismatic staff and strong, visionary leadership," John Lander said. "The group was innovative, always looking for new ways to reach kids.

"I learned quickly that what GIYFC does is pretty simple … but life changing. They care about kids. I love this ministry because God has given me a front-row seat to watch as He transforms the lives of kids."

Board members learn about how GIYFC impacts kids through letters, experiences at camp, and sometimes through personal testimonials. John talked about one particularly impactful story. "It was a young girl who had been abandoned, turned to drugs, and planned to quit school. Her mother was drug addicted, her father was in prison, and her stepfather had sexually abused her. Yet she was willing to tell people like you and me of the love of Jesus.

"I wanted to believe that this story was isolated; these awful things might happen in a big city like LA, Chicago, or NYC, but not Mason City, yet it was happening here. I wondered how I could help. Was there a way I could make a difference?"

As an attorney, he meets adults every day who have been devastated by childhood abuse. "I'm not seeing the child victims—I'm seeing their adult versions, what it might look like for any one of these kids if it were not for GIYFC. Unemployed, unemployable, destitute, imprisoned, untreated, addicted, lost, and discarded by society."

He was invited to speak at a national conference for attorneys about the correlation between childhood sexual abuse and adulthood chronic pain and chronic mental health conditions. In preparing for the program, he found much research on the topic, including the Center for Disease Control and Prevention's study, "Adverse Childhood Experiences" (ACE). This study is one of the most significant investigations of childhood neglect and abuse and later-life health and well-being.

Researchers found that the more trauma a child experiences, the higher the probability that the child will grow up to be an adult with a chronic physical or mental disorder. Examples of traumatic experiences include physical, emotional, and sexual abuse, alcohol or drug abuse in the household, or a having member of the household with mental illness or in prison. In addition, chronic exposure to trauma impacts a child's developing brain. Researchers also concluded that childhood victims of sexual abuse are twice as likely to be jobless, twice as likely to live alone as adults, and 65 percent more likely to suffer from a chronic pain disorder as adults.

What can make a difference? Strong support in a child's life, John said. "What GIYFC does is provide that support system they wouldn't otherwise have."

In his law practice, some of the problems he saw were when "the kids become adults stuck in survival." After recognizing that connection, he set three goals: (1) educate attorneys, (2) educate judges, and (3) "find an organization to put me out of business—that could help these kids before they became adults who needed me. YFC is that organization. They support kids on the battlefield, engaged in survival in real time.

"GIYFC provides a place for kids to feel safe, to feel loved, to feel valued."

Make a Difference for Children around the World

Their hearts were moved when they heard about the mission trip to Zambia in southern Africa. They helped with fundraising and gathered donated clothing and other items for the outgoing mission team.

When the opportunity arose later for another mission trip, it was a foregone conclusion for son Chris and his wife, Morgan. They eagerly spent the next several months planning, organizing a team, fundraising, making girls' dresses, and collecting items to bring to Zambian families.

Their aim was "to make disciples of all nations" by sharing the Good News of Christ's love in schools, orphanages, local gathering areas, and rural bush villages, by providing basic necessities like food, clothing, and Bibles, and assisting with tasks around the

Bible college campus headquarters. They knew it would be a physically, emotionally, and spiritually challenging experience for their team. Zambia is one of the poorest countries in the world, with 10 percent of the population made up of orphaned children. They would be working under the leadership of a Zambian pastor who was an orphan as a child.

To help meet their goals, the group prayed that they would each use their unique gifts to serve others; that they would rely on the Holy Spirit to say and do things that would stir hearts and bring God the most glory; and that the team would have open eyes and hearts to love and care for others.

One of their first tasks was to help serve food to the children at a church. As prepared as the mission team was, nothing could have prepared them for the joyous greeting from the throngs of orphans who ran out to welcome them. Nothing could have prepared them for the gratitude the children expressed. Nothing could have prepared them for their joyful hearts. They had nothing, yet they had everything. They had Jesus's love in their hearts.

Prayers were answered. Life would never be the same.

Son Chris returned a few years later to help construct the Land of Hope, a fifty-acre orphanage and sustainable community in the Zambian bush that provides housing and clean water, produces its own food for the children, and also sells it. Widows feel needed and connected again because they play an essential role as the house mama for their kids. But more than anything, Land of Hope is a sanctuary where children who have lost everything are loved, nurtured, and shepherded into a lifelong relationship with their savior, Jesus. This innovative project, with its mission to "elevate orphans to live out their God-given potential," can serve as a model for helping lift up other needy people in the world. Learn more at www.landofhopeafrica.org.

Make a Difference for America's First Children

"Why are your eyes blue?"

The little three-year-old looked intently at me, tilting his head with emphasis. I was dumbfounded. Maybe he'd never been this close to someone with blue eyes. Finally, I mumbled something profound like, "Well, I guess because my parents had blue eyes. That's a good question." He scooted over, and I hugged him. We sat quietly on the floor, waiting to hear about the next activity.

A few minutes passed.

"Would you come live with us?" he asked with a big grin.

My newfound buddy and I had started our morning as strangers playing basketball together. Then we played tag and, afterward, headed to the crafts room. Later that day, I was surprised to learn that this sweet boy had a reputation as a little terror at the Kids Club.

These kids are descendants of America's first residents, now known as the Sisseton Wahpeton Dakota tribe. My husband, Tom, and I were group leaders for middle and high school students participating in a mission trip in the Lake Traverse, South Dakota, area. The mission organization we joined had established a longtime relationship with community members, serving as a bridge between White and native communities through Kids Club and doing house repair and painting. The goal was respectful service—listen closely, speak carefully, serve humbly, and participate gratefully in what God is already doing in these communities.

Learning the lesser-known history of our nation and its original inhabitants provided a critical context to understand social and racial issues that are prominent on today's reservations. Like other native tribes across the country, their history is one of several broken treaties, accelerated conflict with each new gold rush discovery across the continent, and forced removal and resettlement. Most of our youth were shocked and saddened to learn of the history.

Significant issues remain today. A tribal member and one of the speakers said that the NAACP said relations were worse here than in the Deep South. As the organizers noted, there is a clear economic and social divide between the White and native communities. Although the tribe has made strides to create a job infrastructure, unemployment and poverty are among the worst in the nation. In addition, the opioid crisis struck reservations, like the rest of the country.

I had long been interested in Native American history and culture. But here was a chance to do tangible work projects, provide encouragement and support, help break down stereotypes, and impact our perspectives, organizers said. The work projects included painting, basic construction, and helping staff the Kids Club. My team's first project was to paint houses at the reservation. We drove out into the countryside, past lakes with sizeable homes, and then on to the reservation with blocks of small cookie-cutter houses. Mission leaders told us that the house-painting project was a relatively new initiative, so we shouldn't initiate conversation—but, of course, respond if someone talked to us—and be extra respectful of their property. Our homeowner kindly offered us water. Little children playing in the yard occasionally stopped to watch. "Why are you painting the house?" one of the little girls asked. "Your leader said it would help out," was our reply.

These, hopefully, were small steps forward with no strings attached. "It may be hard to know the impact you make," one of the leaders told us as she thanked everyone for taking their vacation time to help others. But remember that God can work through you.

The staff also told us that God is interested in our personal growth. That became evident as we explored the theme of "storyline" throughout the week: "What if you knew that your story is valuable? Unique? Important? That God's goodness and unfailing love is present through all your highs and lows? While brokenness is often part of your story, it isn't the full story. And how would your story be greater if you knew that God feels this way toward everyone?"

Hey, just a minute! I thought the focus was on the kids, not the leaders.

They told us to start thinking about our own stories—what is your age; where do you live; what are you good at; what are you downright terrible at; what are you proud of; what are you embarrassed about; what do you tend to hide about yourself; if you could change one thing, what would it be; and so on.

Oh my. I thought this was for the kids' personal growth, not mine!

But I should set a good example and start filling this out. Hmmm. If I could change one thing, it would be my feeling of never being enough. But I read on the next page I don't need to hide that and overcompensate for that. Why? Because Jesus already knows every sordid detail of our lives. But He still reaches out to us with love. He accepts us where we are today but doesn't want us to stay there; He wants us to continue to grow.

We got to know other volunteers who were spending their vacations helping others. While our group was painting a house, I noticed that one genial and athletic teen was missing a hand. His mom told me it had happened in a meat grinder accident, such a horrible and scary incident. But she said that their faith had gotten them through it. She noted that experiences like this mission trip focus on helping others, which also boosts his confidence.

One of the other adult chaperones was always the first to get the coffee going early in the morning for the adults. His wife had just been diagnosed with breast cancer shortly before he'd planned to head out on the mission trip. He wanted to stay home with her, but she had insisted he go because helping others would help him deal with the news. Another chaperone's husband had recently passed away, but she was determined to accompany her daughter. Group leaders were energetic college students who came from across the United States and other countries to serve others.

One of our responsibilities was to help local nursing home residents, whether it was playing the piano, helping with projects, or providing a listening ear. One elderly Native American talked about her family's farm in the high country. Her father and mother had worked hard to sustain their family during the seasonal extremes of their homeland. In addition to the planting, harvesting, and animal husbandry chores, one of her favorite memories was gathering wild berries to enjoy and then canning the rest to eat in the winter. Unfortunately, she said those berries aren't plentiful anymore because of the spraying done by the neighboring farmers.

But the government split their family apart when she and her sister were required to attend boarding school in a different part of the state. They were taken away in late summer and didn't see family again until the end of the school year in the spring. She recalled how frightened her younger sister had been when strangers met them at the school. They were the last students to arrive, and no beds were available, so they had to sleep on cots near the kitchen. Months passed before they could sleep in a bed.

The children could only speak English at the boarding school. Teachers punished them if they tried to speak in their native tongue, even with their siblings. They deeply missed their parents and being on the farm, she said.

I asked her how this had impacted her family and sense of community after they could return home. She paused and looked out the window, her dark brown eyes scanning the horizon. Her son died years ago. Her daughter lives several hundred miles away in another city but visits occasionally. Another resident slowly pushed her walker by us, waved, and smiled. "It is good to have some friends at the nursing home," she said, returning the wave.

On the last night of the trip, we provided a community dinner in the city park. We all helped prepare the food and looked forward to serving it. It was a great time to talk with community members and parents of some children who attended Kids Club. One mom talked about how much her children looked forward to Kids Club. It wasn't easy, however, when Kids Club wrapped up for the summer. "Only one week left," she said, looking over her shoulder at her children playing on the swings.

Suddenly, one of the staff members came up to me, followed by a group of kids. "There has been a racial incident with one of your kids," she said. Some of our mission group kids had been playing basketball with local kids when one of the Native American teenagers called one of our teenagers the "N" word, along with some expletives. Our fourteen-year-old thankfully restrained himself in his response to her.

After I said a silent prayer to say the right thing, we told the girl who made the inflammatory comment that she needed to apologize to him in front of the others. We all stood by awkwardly but were grateful to hear her apologize.

"Sometimes we say hurtful comments to others because someone made those comments to us," I said after thanking her. "But that doesn't justify hurting someone else."

I told our young man that I was so sorry this had happened. Maybe someone had called her terrible names, and she didn't want to be alone in her pain. But that sure didn't make it okay. I hugged him. His younger brother stood wide-eyed by his side. He had just been having fun playing basketball with everyone else.

They took off to shoot hoops with another group. Wow. I was heartbroken. We all know kids sometimes say hurtful things to each other; it's part of growing up. But here are two young Black boys spending part of their summer vacation to help Native Americans, and then this happens. Hopefully, the apology will help.

We learned that we would have a washing-of-the-feet ceremony on our last night. Group staff washed the feet of the adult chaperones, who in turn washed the feet of the teenagers. It was a poignant and emotional experience, demonstrating how we are to love and serve one another, as Jesus showed with His disciples on Maundy Thursday.

"Go live your true story," we were told by the mission's group staff. "Be real with Jesus. Your story is no secret to God, so talk with Him about your highs and lows as you go throughout your day. Be real with others. While acknowledging that can be hard, it will help people see God's grace in your life and encourage them to be real with you. Love others through their faults. You don't have to pretend people God puts in your path are perfect. Instead, choose to love people no matter where they're at in their story."

Choose to Love, Not Hate

The weekend we returned home from the mission trip, thirty-five people were murdered and more than forty wounded in mass shootings in El Paso, Texas, and Dayton, Ohio. "Assault on the Nation" and "White Nationalists Pose Urgent Threat" were the headlines in different papers. People reacted with shock, horror, and revulsion across the country.

The El Paso shooter was charged with a hate crime after authorities determined he had posted online that he needed to stop the "Hispanic invasion of Texas." He later allegedly told law enforcement that he targeted Hispanics.

How does someone learn to hate? We can't assume that mass shooters grew up in a family that openly disparaged other races. Research shows a common theme that some of these "angry young men" were bullied at an earlier age. While growing up, they saw a world changing around them, becoming more diverse in ethnicity, culture, and customs. They quietly became indoctrinated into racist theories as they fed on one another's anger in an online ecosystem of hate. The lack of adequate mental health care fuels the fire. Our current political environment of public name-calling, bickering, and sniping also provides that example for our young people.

Can we hear the voice calling for love rather than hate in this frenzied cacophony?

I needed to read what others had written to encourage us in

times of conflict. In his "Loving Your Enemies" sermon delivered on November 17, 1957, at Dexter Avenue Baptist Church in Montgomery, Alabama, Dr. Martin Luther King Jr. made one of his many poignant calls for love over hate. The complete sermon is online at the Martin Luther King Jr. Research and Education Institute at Stanford University.

He cited Matthew chapter 5 to emphasize that we should love our enemies and pray for those who persecute us. He also noted that the willingness to love one another would save all of us, despite its profound difficulty.

> But the wisdom that comes from heaven is first of all pure; then peaceloving, considerate, submissive, full of mercy and good fruit, impartial and sincere. Peacemakers who sow in peace raise a harvest of righteousness. (James 3:17–18 NIV)

The Heavy Lifting

P at yourself on the back.

Look how far you have come already to be stronger and more resilient, to be that better person instead of a bitter person as we face life's inevitable storms.

In a physical fitness plan, the goal often is to lift heavier weights progressively. Similarly, in our My Better Self plan, we are working our way up to the heavy lifting.

So here goes—*heave ho!*

Anger

Acknowledge the anger you may feel about whatever storm or tragedy has befallen you or your family.

Anger makes many of us nervous and scared, and it feels so uncomfortable. Some folks, including me, would prefer to bury those feelings, ignore them, and hope they disappear. Plus, we have so much public anger and outrage now; why encourage this for someone trying to become their better self?

But there are lessons to learn from all of our emotions as we strive to improve ourselves. Properly channeled, the energy of anger can help us make changes. On the other hand, unacknowledged anger can implode, destroying us from the inside. It can explode into violence against others.

So here is my acknowledgment of how I felt about my sister's breast cancer.

It was sorrow, fear, and then anger.

There was anger that doctors missed diagnosing her until it was too late, that her life was cut short, and that she had to suffer so much. I even felt anger that the color representing breast cancer was pink instead of red. We may try to make this hideous, brutal, and painful disease more palatable by masking it in pink and ribbons, but it should be red to symbolize the insidiousness of cancer.

We were all shocked, sad, and angry when we learned how Sue's doctors flatly made mistakes and then chose their HMO profits over Sue's health. Of course, anyone can make a mistake, but how dare they put profits over my sister's well-being? But that anger could have consumed us like cancer.

So Sue, her husband, and our families all chose to focus on Sue's care and our time together. The "red" color had shifted to another emotion: love one another today instead of waiting until tomorrow.

Because then we can move on to ...

Forgiveness

Forgiveness is the next heavy lift as we build our My Better Self muscles.

Most world religions include teachings on forgiveness. Scholars, theologians, and others have written countless volumes to help each generation grapple with what it means to forgive. Learning about it is one thing. But how do we truly forgive ourselves or someone else?

On a personal level, I berated myself in the months and years after my sister's diagnosis for not being able to change her prognosis of metastatic breast cancer.

On a broader level, how do families of the 9/11 victims find forgiveness for such a tragedy? Most did not have "final conversations." Countless people wandered the streets posting pictures of their loved ones, hoping to find out if they were dead or alive. Or how can someone in targeted groups like the Jews in Rhodes, Greece, or Native Americans forgive?

> For if you forgive men when they sin against you, your heavenly Father will also forgive you. But if you do not forgive men their sins, your Father will not forgive your sins. (Matthew 6:14–15 NIV)

> Then Peter came to Jesus and asked, "Lord, how many times shall I forgive my brother when he sins against me? Up to seven times?" Jesus answered, "I tell you, not seven times, but seventy-seven times." (Matthew 18:21–22 NIV)

Surrender and Peace

Most Bible scholars interpret Jesus saying "seventy-seven times" to forgive others as symbolic because we are to forgive without limit.

Admittedly, I was still wrestling with forgiving myself and Sue's doctors when sister Sue strongly encouraged us to take a spring break trip to the desert southwest as a family.

We drove our rented Ford Explorer along the dusty New Mexico road, past brown adobe houses with beehive-like bread ovens in the front yard. Soon, the sprawling Sangre de Christo Mountains came into view, cradling the ancient Taos Pueblo.

We toured the multistoried adobe buildings that members of the Taos tribe have continuously inhabited for more than one thousand years. Now a UNESCO World Heritage site, the culture and history have fascinated me since my college anthropology professor enthusiastically described it.

The tour guide explained that throughout recent centuries, conquering Spaniards, Mexicans, and then American settlers forced their cultures on the ancient pueblo village, often resulting in bloody conflict. For example, Taos Indians were leaders in the great Pueblo Revolt of 1680 against the Spanish. But the revolt was crushed, and land grants split Indian lands and cut off food and water resources.

Later, the United States government's occupation of Taos pueblo and other present-day New Mexico areas led to an insurrection by Hispano (Hispanic New Mexicans) and Pueblo allies in 1847. Following the murder of New Mexico Territorial Governor Charles Bent and six others, federal troops headed to the pueblo because they believed rebels were taking refuge inside the church. But the Taos guide said it was primarily women and children seeking protection there. Nevertheless, troops battered the church for over two days with their Howitzer cannons. The militia then set fire to what remained.

Fragments of the church foundation provide a border to what is now a cemetery. One of the tourists pulled the guide aside as others in the group took photographs of the church remnants. "Aren't you just so mad at what has happened to your people over the years?" he asked. "The governments, the church, society ..."

"What good would it do to be mad?" the guide responded. Instead, she explained what the tribal council was doing to provide new opportunities for young people.

These descendants of the ancient Anasazi still embrace their fundamental values of living in harmony with the natural and human world. A critical step to retain that value was the 1970 return by the federal government of 48,000 acres of mountain land, including their sacred Blue Lake. The federal government claimed it in 1906 to become part of National Forest lands.

After seeing the pueblo, we were looking forward to experiencing the surrounding land, which is open only to Taos Indians and best explored by horseback. After a few more turns on the gravel road, we saw the Taos Indian Horse Ranch sign. I reread the horse ranch brochure. "Finest old tradition … Exclusive access into Indian country. Lots of mountains. Your heart will sing." I was sold.

Horseback riding had become a Lovell family vacation staple. I cheerfully promoted trail horse rides because imagining ourselves in the Wild West was fun. I also knew that we would likely get plodding trail horses, and even I could handle one of those. But as our son got older and the horses faster, my old childhood fear of being bucked off and trampled by a thousand-pound creature resurfaced.

The office, store, and home for the Taos Indian Ranch was an adobe building. "Come right on in," said Sandi "Hoofbeats" Gomez, co-owner of the ranch. She said customers come from all over the country with all riding abilities, sizing us up while smiling a toothless grin. Sandi leaned back in her desk chair, surrounded by a fax machine and personal computer inside the adobe home. "We'll soon be getting our website up," she said, noting that God has been good to them, bringing them more customers in recent years.

But it hasn't always been easy, Sandi said, turning away to cover a smoker's hack. It's not been that many years that townspeople felt they should pay an Indian man half what they would pay a White man. She met Cesario "Stormstar" Gomez, a Taos Indian, out in San Francisco. She thought he was Italian, Sandi said, with a mischievous wink and a belly laugh.

"Take off your earrings and remove your necklaces; I've seen them ripped right off people," she warned me after I signed the waiver. I hesitantly made my way out to the corral and hauled myself onto the saddle. Our guide, Bernard, took us at a slow pace, peacefully traveling along the ancient horse trail through the pines into the Sangre de Christos.

As a boy, Bernard and his friends spent their summer days riding horses far back into the mountains, he said. While beautiful, it can be challenging to earn a living in this high mountain desert village, Bernard added. He'd made good money elsewhere as a fire jumper. But that was a dangerous job. And the commanders were often more concerned about controlling the fires than the safety of the firefighters. So, he returned to the pueblo to make a living for his family.

A gentle breeze blew through the pinion trees, whispering of generations who had traveled this path before us. We stopped to gaze out on the sprawling plateau. "See that?" Our guide pointed to a tornado-like dirt spiral near the Rio Grande River gorge. "They call them desert spirits," Bernard said. We watched as they danced across the desert. And then it was time to head home.

We returned the next day to the horse ranch, hoping we could go for a leisurely sunset ride. But as we stood in her office, Sandi looked us over again and suggested we do the "Spirit Ride" for experienced riders. "Bernard said your psyches seemed ready," Sandi said. "It just might be your head that limits you."

"Does that mean we get to gallop really fast?" our son, Chris, said as he leaped off the chair and ran out the door. He and young Sunbow, Stormstar and Sandi's granddaughter, were ready to saddle up. My husband, Tom, grinned from ear to ear. My heart began to pound, my pulse raced, and my palms began to sweat. Childhood fears were mounting up

"You can have my favorite horse," Stormstar told me kindly as he hoisted me up on the saddle. I tightly cinched my cowboy hat string under my chin.

Some of their family members were instrumental in convincing the federal government to return their sacred Blue Lake and surrounding acres to the tribe in 1970. It took over sixty-four years and even the help of President Nixon to conclude this landmark Native American case. Taos oral tradition holds that the entire tribe, except the aged or infirm, treks forty miles roundtrip to the Blue Lake for personal renewal each year.

"We'll have to make some good time to get the ride in before the sun sets," Bernard said. We reached an open field, and he asked if everyone was ready to gallop. "Lean back in the saddle. Let yourself feel the rhythm of the horse," Bernard said. "Trust that she will know the way." We gave the command, and the horses were off. I clung to the saddle horn for dear life. My body bobbed like a ragdoll tied to a bucking bronco.

As we finally slowed to a walk, Bernard explained that he liked to teach people to ride bareback so they learned to trust the horse's rhythm. We wound our way through the foothills and up a canyon. A fox peered out from behind a pine tree. The dogs took after it, yowling in hot pursuit. We galloped again, this time through the pinion and cedar trees. The rich cedar aroma filled my nostrils as my horse brushed against a bough. We stopped to look at the panorama before us.

Bernard knew the ancient Taos language, passed down in oral tradition through the generations. Kids today are not as interested in learning it, he said wistfully, flipping his long black ponytail on his back. But it is better in schools now than it was in earlier years. Previously, children were required to leave their families and the pueblo at age five to be taught in Bureau of Indian Affairs–run schools. If children spoke their native Taos language, teachers solidly rapped their hands with a ruler. "We quickly learned that we were not to speak our language or discuss our traditions," he said.

But as an adult, he was grateful to participate in some of those traditions. To live on the reservation land, one must be a Taos Indian and join the ancient societies' sacred rites.

"See all the new growth on the pinion trees?" Bernard said. "We have had good rains this year, and for that we are grateful." He recalled the year of the drought. He was on a hunting trip back in the mountains. Even though he had water with him, he felt he should not drink it because he knew the surrounding trees did not have enough water. "I know that sounds funny, but can you understand what I mean?" We are all interconnected.

The horses paused, and we watched the sun begin to set on the Rio Grande plateau. We were far from the constant news reports of road bombings and terrorist kidnappings and beheadings in the Middle East. We seemed removed from the horror of the 9/11 terrorist attack. "When the terrorists attacked the Trade Towers, I prayed for our country," Bernard said. "We pray for peace for all humankind. And I pray for your own peace."

I recalled a comment by a woman who left a stressful career as an international airline stewardess to become a massage therapist. "Passengers used to always be in such a rush and so angry," she said. "After 9/11, they instead were always filled with fear."

My heart ached as I thought of my sister, whose breast cancer was seeping through her bones and into her organs. Yet, despite her physical pain and mental anguish, she focused on being grateful every day. She loved repeating the British prime minister's inspiring directive to Londoners to never give up despite the relentless Nazi air attacks night after night. I was the fearful one—afraid that her body would wear out before the next treatment was available, fearful of what life would be without her.

As we wound our way through the foothills, Bernard's words resonated. Despite the history of pain and suffering, Taos Indians, Hispanics, and Anglos now coexist in the same community. We can see what matters despite loss and tragedy or sometimes because of it. We can face our fears—big and small—and one another with courage, love, and compassion.

As we rode out of the mountains at sunset, there was a brilliant rose, yellow, and pink palette in the New Mexico sky. It embraced and surrounded us with intensity like it had so many before us. I could now feel the smooth, steady rhythm of my cantering horse.

Maybe I could stop white-knuckling it, clinging so tightly, needing to control this thousand-pound spirited animal I was riding.

I loosened the reins, leaned back in the saddle, and felt the rhythmic cadence of the horse. Bernard's words, my sister's words—forgive each other, love one another—all resonated with the twilight. No more discussion, but faith. I surrendered to trust that all was well.

Reconciliation in Rwanda

Their important work arose from the ashes of the 1994 genocide in Rwanda and neighboring Burundi.

As many as 800,000 people were slaughtered, and millions of refugees became homeless as ethnic hostility exploded and neighbors took up arms against neighbors in eastern Africa. Arthur and Molly Rouner of Minneapolis were invited in 1995 by World Vision to partner with eastern African leaders to explore how to help heal such deeply wounded countries. Some organizations provided practical support for medical clinics, wells, and schools, which were all desperately needed.

> "Yet if people are in conflict, they will end up fighting over the clinic, the well, and the school," Molly Rouner said. "So our work of reconciliation was birthed.

> It was very early morning. Our room in one of the few functioning hotels in Rwanda had a small balcony. Molly stood there a long time, looking out into the morning mist of Rwanda. "On that first day," she confessed, "I stared at the beautiful hills of Rwanda, that had such devastating evil in the awful killing time, and I asked God over and over, why have you brought me to this place? I have no skills, no expertise to help these people. And He said to me then and repeatedly in the month that

followed, "I have brought you here to go to your knees before them, to ask the forgiveness of these people for what your own people of the West did, to divide them from each other."

In the days that followed, some thirty people from the Tutsi and Hutu staff of the Protestant Council of Churches of Rwanda gathered, and she did just that. She pulled out a chair, placed it in the center of the room, bowed down, and knelt at the chair, waiting. One by one they began to surround her, lay hands on her, and prayed for her ... the very forgiveness she had asked.

Something strange and wonderful happened by the power of the Spirit. A hand of healing touched that whole community through a simple heartfelt action of confession and repentance.

After the genocide, there were plenty of ideas of what reconciliation was, and people from the West were pouring in to conduct seminars and workshops, lectures, and teaching on reconciliation. Suddenly there was another answer. The way into the heart was not through information or explanation—what was needed was to find a way for the experience of healing to happen.

This was the beginning of our call to be reconcilers. (Pilgrim Center for Reconciliation, Minneapolis, Minnesota)

More than twenty-five thousand people have found new life, according to one of the facilitators in Rwanda. That has led to restored communities and hope for the future.

Their reconciliation work has spread into other eastern African countries. In addition, reconciliation courses and retreats are also offered in the United States (www.pilgrimcenter.org).

"The wounded, angry heart is a universal issue," according to a Pilgrim Center newsletter.

Fred

Although my friends and I were freshmen in high school, our collective concept of what was funny was stuck in a sixth-grade mentality at best.

One of our pastimes was to look for anything that might be a bit unusual about our teachers. Our freshman English instructor, Fred Wilson, had what we thought had to be a toupee, so our attention often was not on conjugations but on whether his wig might fall off that day. We chuckled as he passionately read *Romeo and Juliet* in a dramatic baritone voice. We didn't chuckle so much about how often we got sent to the principal's office just because we giggled uncontrollably about something.

Sadly, we weren't the only ones doing this. But by the time I was a senior, however, I noticed that he was an excellent speech coach—I won a state speech contest under his mentoring. He encouraged us to be creative and share our passions with others. I hoped for a chance to ask for his forgiveness for my earlier immaturity. But I was too embarrassed to take action.

I hadn't thought much about Fred after attending college, working in Oregon, and moving to Minnesota. But we eventually returned to our hometown, and years later, I saw an article in the newspaper announcing that someone named Fred Wilson was coming to Clear Lake as part of a speaking tour on forgiveness. This mild-mannered, retired English teacher told his story about being on death's doorstep after being shot in an Omaha, Nebraska, shopping mall in December 2007. Fred got a department store job as a second career because he loved helping people. But one day, a man suddenly brandished an assault rifle and began shooting randomly. In the worst mass slaying in Nebraska history, the gunman killed five men and three women and injured five, including Fred. The shooter eventually turned the gun on himself.

Fred, meanwhile, was bleeding out and had no pulse after being rushed to the hospital. From his hospital bed, he expressed gratitude for those who'd helped him and condolences to the families of his beloved coworkers. Wilson told a reporter on a local television station that he held no anger toward the shooter and that he wanted to be a better person who appreciates life more.

While speaking in Clear Lake, he emphasized the importance of family. He marveled at how his family all rallied around him after this tragedy. "It's amazing, the impact we have on one another, and we don't realize it until something like this happens," he said. "It's like I have a second chance."

Fred suffered permanent disabilities, despite many surgeries. Yet he publicly urged people to learn how to forgive others and "to live your life without the burden of hatred and animosity ... We are faced with the never-ending choice to become the wounded or to heal."

"We need to be caring and forgiving," he told a reporter of *Metro Magazine* in Omaha in 2009. "We are all mortals, and everyone will die someday. We don't know how long we are given. We just need to cherish our moments. We assume as we step into our days thinking that we'll be fine, but people have heart attacks, falls, or traffic accidents ... I'm so blessed to still be able to have the opportunity to live my days and see the seasons and holidays. Not one day goes by without my saying 'Thank you, God, thank you, Jesus.'"

Forgiveness Without Limits

We have been taught to forgive continuously, without limits, even with that most challenging one – ourselves.

Sometimes we think we have moved on but are unexpectedly

jabbed with a painful reminder and need to revisit the forgiveness stages.

For many, it could be childhood incidents like physical or verbal abuse, parental addictions, mental illness, or seemingly innocuous "stupid kid" comments. I was reminded of the impact of ongoing criticisms when I found this note from a friend in sister Sue's boxes of papers: "Happy Birthday Sooz! Once when I complimented you on some jewelry, you said that you were trying to wear it to show that you value yourself. So I thought, hmm, if I give Sooz jewelry maybe she'll understand how dearly I value her. I hope so anyway! Love you, —"

If Sue had valued herself more, maybe Sue would have advocated for herself with the doctors. And for Sue, that was a matter of life and death.

Like many of us, we three sisters seemed to lack a basic sense of "somebodiness," a basic belief in oneself, as Dr. Martin Luther King Jr. described to a group of junior high students in his "What Is Your Life's Blueprint?" speech in Philadelphia in 1967. It is essential that each of us has a deep belief in our dignity and self-worth and feel that our life has ultimate significance, he told them.

We could tell ourselves to buck up and forget it. But harboring difficult issues keeps us prisoners of the past and can mean repeating that cycle with the next generation. Instead, we can acknowledge an issue, learn how to forgive, and then take responsibility for letting it go. It frees us to live in the present.

I chose to end the cycles I saw and try to remind my family, with words and actions, of how much they are loved. And I ask each day that God forgives me for the times I fall short.

Mom

Who among us lives our life according to "our plan"? Mom's life undoubtedly was not what she had planned.

Mom was smart, hardworking, and well-read. And a planner.

As an only child, she was close to her parents. She also felt the pressure to succeed but not make a big deal of it since she lived in a small town. As kids, we enjoyed looking at her college graduation and wedding photos. She was beautiful, with an Ingrid Bergman–like look and smile and coiffed shoulder-length hair. She got top-notch grades in college and worked for a large corporation after graduating. After marrying, she opted to be a full-time mom but was diligent in her roles on the boards of family businesses.

As the family travel planner, she ensured that we kids learned about new places and cultures. Whether it was a trip to a museum or reading about the history of the next destination, we could stretch our imaginations. But helping three kids pack, boarding the pets, and listening to our "You are in my space" complaints en route in the station wagon wasn't easy. There were the stops for the child who regularly got car sick. Plus, she had to pay attention to our route to ensure that Dad, the driver, was not trying another infamous "shortcut."

Mom was always busy at home and was an active community volunteer. The rare times that we kids saw her relax were when we were in the woods or when she played the piano.

She bandaged our scraped knees and cared for us through bouts of measles, tonsillitis, Sue's ruptured appendix, and my concussions. One of my most tender childhood memories is of Mom patiently holding a washcloth on my forehead to bring down a chickenpox fever.

As years passed, Mom's criticisms of herself and us became more frequent. As angelic and well-meaning as we all were, raising three kids who were close in age with a workaholic husband was tough. As an only child, Mom did not understand that bantering among siblings was normal.

My sisters and I reached adulthood, graduated from college, married, and lived elsewhere. But Mom's life changed dramatically when her healthy father suffered a major stroke and remained incapacitated until his passing away. Taking care of her mom was the next priority. After Gram passed away, Mom and Dad took some trips and spent time in warmer winter climates. Dad never officially retired, but his work and traveling with Mom ended after doctors diagnosed his unusual behavior as Alzheimer's, for which there is no cure. So Mom cared for him at home until he started running out into the busy street without looking.

Dad's health issues started while daughter Sue was battling breast cancer. After Dad passed away, Mom could travel more often to see Sue. Thank God for those precious times we could gather, acknowledge past hardships and understand that life includes pain for every human being. "I can't correct the past," Sue said during one of those conversations. "I can choose not to be bitter or angry. I can choose to accept all that has happened and go from here. I can live in the present and enjoy my day." Those gatherings were when Sue told us what she had learned: "I would have loved more, forgiven more, and been closer to my family." Those gatherings opened the door for each family member to help create a written "This is a Prayer for Our Susan" to let Sue know how much we loved her and help her see how she had positively impacted the world with her one-of-a-kind abilities. And those gatherings led to the three sisters compiling our long lists of gratefulness for the many things Mom had done for us and others.

After Sue died, we all tried to find a "new normal." We got together often, and Mom was a regular with us at grandson Chris's events. But Midwestern winters can be harsh, so my sister Sarah and I encouraged Mom to consider a warmer climate trip. It took a few years before she agreed to travel with a friend to California. But after just about a week, she fell and broke her hip. Despite surgery and physical therapy, she never walked on her own again.

A very determined, independent person, Mom had more than a broken hip. Her heart had been broken earlier by losing her husband and daughter.

Thankfully, there were ways to help provide some comfort.

A good friend gave Mom her favorite book of daily devotions to read. We made reading that dog-eared book Mom's morning and evening ritual for the two of us. Mom always had her tiny spiral notebook handy to write down the most meaningful ones.

And then more physical comfort came in the form of a four-legged furry critter. It was Thanksgiving Day, and we had finished cleaning up the dishes at Mom's house when I heard a faint *meoooow*. A cat peered through Mom's sliding glass door into her warm house. Tom saw the plaintive cat and quickly said, "Do *not* open that door!" He said it with the conviction of one who already had a stowaway cat as a family member.

I worried about that poor kitty out in the cold, but I resisted my urge to open the door. Chris and I started walking back to our house and soon realized the cat was following us. We tried to ignore it. *Meoooow, meow*. We dashed to the house. But it is hard to outrun a cat.

Poor thing. We'll give the cat some water and food and keep it in the heated garage for the night. And find her a nice little bed. Oh, that poor little kitty lost an ear. She's had a tough life already. We'll look for her owners in the morning.

Long story short, no one claimed her. But we already had two pets. I recalled Mom's stories about her pet dogs while growing up, plus she was always great about letting us kids have dogs and other pets. She previously commented that it was silly for people her age to have a pet. But I asked her anyway; she said maybe.

I brought the cat to Mom's house and intended to put her gently on the floor. But the cat leaped out of my arms, bounded onto Mom's bed, and lay beside Mom, freely offering love and companionship. And that is where Cali the calico cat nestled days and nights, snuggling with my mom.

We were so grateful that Mom could stay in her home with wonderful caregivers after she broke her hip. Sadly, she could not walk unassisted, but family and friends could visit, we could go for car rides, and she could look out on the lake and watch the changing seasons. A few years later, our son Chris had a chance to take the annual high school trip to Washington, DC, and the leader asked us to chaperone. We were concerned that Mom was slowing down, but she was adamant that we go. We called every day with updates. After we returned, Mom was weaker but wanted to see pictures and hear all about the trip. My birthday also was that week, and she insisted that we celebrate.

Sister Sarah (Soz) was able to come that week, and we took turns keeping Mom company and then catching a little shut-eye. One morning after our caregiver checked her vital signs, I went back into Mom's bedroom. Her vital signs were good, and Mom was resting peacefully. I patted her hand, and she patted back.

I looked out the window at the lake, thinking I might see someone passing by on a paddleboard or in a sailboat. But, instead, something had perched near the window. I exclaimed excitedly, "Look, Mom! It's a dove. It's God's love. It's God's love, Mom."

Suddenly, Mom became restless. I called out to sister Sarah. "We love you. We love you so much." And then our mama passed on.

Years later, I discovered some small sheets of paper tucked away in one of Mom's Bibles. Mom had torn the sheets from one of her tiny spiral notepads. Yes, it was Mom's handwriting. But it was very light and hard to read. She had difficulty pressing down on the paper at this stage in her life. It read:

10 p.m. – holding our family in the light of God's love. Soz Sue Jan

Strengthening the Core

We are making significant progress on the more challenging parts of our My Better Self plan to help build our resiliency and contribute to a better world. Yet something is missing.

It has to do with our core. (Thankfully, not our physical stomach "core," which, for me, involves mystery muscles that fossilized long ago.)

But it is about that all-important muscle—the heart. In our ongoing quest to become better people, build that resilience, and make it through life's challenges, this organ needs to stay pumped up for life in every aspect.

While marketers today promote the heart as the symbol of emotion and love, the ancients viewed it differently. To the ancient Hebrews, the heart ensured physical life but also was the center of human thought and spiritual life—where we make choices.

Guard Your Heart

Guard your heart above all else, for it is the source of life.
—Proverbs 4:23

A heart of stone is hard to resuscitate.

As we all grow older and experience hardships and broken promises, it is easy to slip into having a hardened heart. But if we don't pay attention, each injustice we think we have suffered can become a piece of emotional baggage that gets heavier and heavier until it weighs us down.

Granted, if someone breaks our hearts in a relationship, it will take time to mend it. Losing a loved one to a disease or a tragic accident is searingly painful. But a long-term fixation on our pain can become quicksand that entraps. We need to remember that others have felt this pain as well. And have faith in our restoration.

Restoration

I had taken Sue's suggestion about restoration literally. She and I felt strongly about restoring the Lone Tree Point Nature Area, which had prairies, wetlands, and other natural habitats, to help improve lake water quality and create some balance within the natural world. People who never cared about prairies and their vital role in the ecosystem now have a better understanding as they enjoy a ritual of biking through the restored prairie to enjoy the ever-changing panorama of different seasons.

But beyond physical world restoration, Sue's illness provided an opportunity to do the work of restoring relationships even amid our sadness. Mom and Sue restored their relationship. Loving each other and spending time together became a priority. Sue began to realize her intrinsic value.

And this restoration focus is even more impactful. It is about the restoration and deepening of our relationship with our Creator. It is about a promise made long ago:

> And I will give you a new heart, and a new spirit
> I will put within you. And I will remove the heart
> of stone from your flesh and give you a heart of
> flesh. And I will put my Spirit within you and

cause you to walk in my statutes and be careful to obey my rules. (Ezekiel 36:26–28 NIV)

As a child, it was easy to sing, "Yes, Jesus loves me." But along life's journey, I've done some dumb things; I have fallen so short of what I could have done; I have been angry at others because I felt mistreated; I have thought I was the one with the answers. The list goes on. Despite this, my pastor says God wants a relationship with me.

With me? Why would the God of this universe care about me?

I recalled Pastor Thom Christian's signature signoff: "Unworthy but His." I understand the unworthy part. But His? We all can try to hide our insecurities and faults. But as our mission trip leaders pointed out, Jesus knows all our flaws and mistakes.

Busted.

And yet He still reaches out with "unfailing love" (Psalm 32:10 NIV).

Is grasping that notion—that we have a God who cares about us—an essential part of becoming a better person?

If so, how do we restore that relationship? Pastor Harlan suggested trying a typical method for deepening relationships with people—spending time together. But how dare we do that with an omniscient, all-powerful God?

Start by Reading the Bible

I grew up having the Bible read to me and later reading the Bible myself, usually before going to sleep at night. I must admit, however, that when I was in elementary school, I focused on the "lite" version, the Sunday PIX comics and the heroes of the Bible stories. A TV series, *Davey and Goliath*, hit home as Davey and his talking dog faced different moral conflicts. He didn't always make the right first choice, but thanks to the guidance of his parents and teachers, he always learned a valuable life lesson in the end. And in middle school, I loved my confirmation class because there was so much to learn and discuss.

But in my high school years, my confirmation Bible gathered dust as I saw the hypocrisy of some TV evangelists who filled their personal coffers, lived lavish lifestyles, and violated their own dictums with scandals. I met folks who advertised themselves as Christians but lived mean-spirited lives. Learning about the persecutions and injustices during the Inquisition and the violence and ruthlessness of the Crusades was disheartening.

Maybe our sociopolitical climate had an impact too. I was in that impressionable middle school age in 1968. I remember the shock of seeing humanity's underbelly as TV provided a front-row seat to the Vietnam War, the assassinations of Martin Luther King Jr. and Bobby Kennedy, and college students killed while protesting the Vietnam War.

Even though I attended a church-affiliated college, it was not cool to merely regurgitate what we learned in a church in earlier years. When I became a newspaper reporter, my colleagues and I competed to do the news stories from the cop beat or about politics. The church page was for lightweights.

I attended church regularly but more out of a sense of responsibility than desire. I felt that something was missing, for sure. But I stayed busy and kept my head down.

And then along came a new pastor and his Bible study. And the Bible came back to life. He helped us understand that although the cultural context was different, the people in the Bible were grappling with many of the same challenges and fears that we are today. He proclaimed that the Bible is a love letter. And that God is a loving God.

The Bible doesn't gloss over the cruelties, selfishness, and pitfalls of being human. Instead, it chronicles humanity—warts and all. After all, God selected many biblical heroes despite their weaknesses. And others, like Paul, an infamous persecutor of Christians, were chosen for redemption.

Paul's remarkable story sprang to life when we traveled to some of the sites of Paul's mission trips in Greece and Turkey in AD 49–52. On our second day in Athens, we hiked up to the Areopagus, where Paul preached his most dramatic and fully recorded speech to some Athenians. As recorded in the book of Acts 17:16–34, Paul said they should worship one Creator God instead of the many gods they enshrined throughout Athens. Later, in Turkey, we walked among the ruins of Ephesus, a prosperous city and the location of the Temple of Artemis, one of the most revered Greek gods.

These were both large commercial centers with economies built on the worship of Greek gods and governed by the Roman empire, which decreed that Caesar was the only king. It would have taken God-given courage to share Jesus's message in these cities.

Prayer

Another impactful way to restore our relationship with our Creator is through prayer.

"I want you girls always to remember the power of prayer," my gram said when I was at her bedside on a night we both feared might be her last.

When sister Sue was so sick, I would head downstairs after everyone was in bed, get on my knees, and pray over and over to God for a miracle. I read and reread the scripture sections about miracles. And then I prayed about that. Maybe, I worried, I hadn't prayed enough. Or I hadn't asked others to pray for us.

Our prayers don't always result in what *we* think should happen. But prayer is imperative to deepen our relationship with God, Pastor Harlan noted, because it helps establish an honest relationship and a genuine attitude of trust and dependence on

God. Pray to God as though He is your best friend, Pastor Harlan said.

What? Pray to the Creator of the universe as though He is my best friend? With all the war, hunger, conflict, disease, and natural disasters in the world, why would God care about my minor issues?

Repeat: the Creator of the universe cares about each one of us.

After thinking about it a bit, I guess I have always prayed, at least for as long as I can remember. I recalled the comfort that surrounded me as a little girl when I prayed, like having someone pull a warm, soft blanket over me. How could I recapture that?

But as adults, how are we to communicate with the Creator of the universe? There are bazillions of books written about praying—techniques, structure, correct words to use, acronyms to help remember, and so forth. But this is the God who sees us in secret. There is no pretense. Yikes.

"Prayer is not a magic wand, a first aid kit, or a religious duty that we must perform to avoid the 'bad list,'" Pastor Harlan said. But it does require dedicated commitment. Here are some of his suggestions:

Devise a plan to make prayer a habit. To whatever extent it is possible, set aside a time and determine a quiet place.

> For when you pray, do not be like the hypocrites, for they love to pray standing in the synagogues and on the street corners to be seen by men ... But when you pray, go into your room, close the door, and pray to your Father, who is unseen. Then your Father, who sees what is done in secret, will reward you. (Matthew 6:5–7 NIV)

Be honest with yourself about why you are praying. Are you just asking for more for yourself? "If a man shuts his ears to the cry of the poor, he too will cry out and not be answered." (Proverbs 21:13 NIV)

"We are blessed so that others may be blessed," Pastor Harlan said. We need to ask forgiveness for the wrongs we have done, and we also need to forgive others. "Nothing will kill your prayers faster than resentment against someone else," he said.

Frequent and sincere prayers of thankfulness make it harder to clutter our minds with negative thoughts or complaints. A straightforward way to start is with gratefulness for what we otherwise may take for granted—a warm shower, clothes to wear, and food to eat. And then continue it throughout the day. Post "In everything, give thanks" signs in visible areas in your house or office.

> Be joyful always; pray continuously; give thanks
> in all circumstances, for this is God's will for you
> in Christ Jesus. (1 Thessalonians 5:23 NIV)

If you have a favorite prayer, post it on your refrigerator. My mom had posted one of Gram's favorites: "Dear Father, help us to remember that we are the channels of thy power. That thy work is done with our hands, and thy word spread with our mouths and our examples. Give us strength, courage, and inspiration to further thy work here and in all parts of the world."

Prayer and reading the Bible are essential pathways to help awaken our hearts and understand the importance of the next step.

Choose to Surrender

As children growing up, we all heard the "if at first you don't succeed, try, try again." My parents and grandparents continually instilled the idea of "work hard and don't give up." Persistence and tenacity are generally considered admirable traits in our society.

So, choose to surrender? Perhaps we might be forced to surrender someday, but why would we choose to do this?

At some point in our lives, we begin to realize that humans do not control everything that impacts us. That realization is why I have a picture of a windsurfer in my office with the inscription, "We cannot control the wind ... but we can adjust the sails." And I would not have imagined that riding a horse could provide an important lesson. But when I finally relinquished trying to control a thousand-pound thoroughbred and just fell into the rhythm of the horse's gallop, absorbed the glory of a panoramic New Mexican sunset, and, for a short while at least, accepted that I could not control my sister's health situation, I felt an indescribable serenity.

The Serenity Prayer, which has become part of the twelve-step programs to help treat addiction, has helped millions sort out what we can control or cannot:

> God, give us grace to accept with serenity
> the things that cannot be changed,
> Courage to change the things
> which should be changed,
> and the wisdom to distinguish
> the one from the other.

And here is the second, less well-known part of the prayer that theologian Reinhold Niebuhr wrote:

> Living one day at a time,
> Enjoying one moment at a time,
> Accepting hardship as a pathway to peace,
> Taking, as Jesus did,
> This sinful world as it is,
> Not as I would have it,

Trusting that You will make all things right,
If I surrender to Your will,
So that I may be reasonably happy in this life,
And supremely happy with You forever in the next.
Amen.

Even King Solomon, considered the wisest, wealthiest, and most powerful man in his ancient world, wrestled with his purpose and how to have a meaningful life. In his later years, he acknowledged that material possessions do not provide life purpose, scholars have noted. Despite his power over so many, he also wrote about how each person is subject to uncontrollable events:

There is a time for everything,
And a season for every activity under heaven:
A time to be born and a time to die,
A time to plant and a time to uproot,
A time to kill and a time to heal,
A time to tear down and a time to build,
A time to weep and a time to laugh,
A time to mourn and a time to dance,
A time to scatter stones and a time to gather them,
A time to embrace and a time to refrain,
A time to search and a time to give up,
A time to keep and a time to throw away,
A time to tear and a time to mend,
A time to be silent and a time to speak,
A time to love and a time to hate,
A time for war and a time for peace. (Ecclesiastes 3:1–8)

He concluded that faith in the eternal God is the only way to find purpose and meaning. Therefore, obey God, trust God, and love God.

Choosing to surrender is not just meekly waving a small white flag. It's a full-hearted, *Thy will be done, not my will. I put my complete trust and faith in You to show me the way and to obey Your commands.*

Trust in the Lord with all your heart and lean not on your own understanding.

In all your ways acknowledge him,

And he will make your paths straight. (Proverbs 3:5–6 NIV)

The Great Storm

A strong core is also vital during a worldwide storm.

We heard about this global storm as it traveled across the continents to North America. Within months, COVID-19 was the number one cause of death in the United States.

It was highly contagious. And often asymptomatic. Unknowingly, my very presence could cause another person to contract the illness and die. And fiendishly, it was spreading by our own breath.

How will we choose to react to this—with fear, skepticism, selfishness, or anger? Or will we be the calm voice in the boat in this storm, ensuring that all are wearing their life jackets as we hunker down together for safe passage?

New York City hospitals became "apocalyptic," as they were overwhelmed with patients and lacked equipment, protection, and staff. Outside, row upon row of refrigerator trucks lined up to serve as temporary morgues for all the bodies, the unidentified destined for an unmarked wooden box and mass burial. As it spread across the country, we could no longer hug our loved ones despite everyone's increased need for a reassuring human touch. "Essential services" were defined, resulting in business closures and sudden layoffs.

"We're all in this together" became the maxim as neighbors

checked on neighbors, volunteers organized food pantries, and musicians gave free concerts to inspire others. We saw unsung workers like home health aides and bus drivers become heroes overnight.

But as the worldwide storm persisted, it became clear that we weren't all in the same boat. The painful separation from family members in hospitals or nursing homes was heartbreaking. Conflict arose on vaccinations and wearing masks. Fatality numbers became personal as our local numbers rose. "It is a raging fire looking for human wood to burn," said one virus expert. Then, to add fuel to this fire, television viewers worldwide saw the horrifying death of George Floyd and subsequent outrage and protests.

Yet, within a few months, our nation paused for self-reflection during a funeral service for civil rights icon John Lewis. He was a young man in the crowd of Negroes beaten back by state and local police on "Bloody Sunday" in 1965 in Selma, Alabama. An officer cracked John Lewis's skull with a nightstick that day, but Lewis continued to address injustice throughout his life as a congressman. State police saluted his flag-draped casket on a horse-drawn caisson as the procession crossed the famed Edmund Pettus Bridge in July 2020.

Perhaps those moments of a respectful pause provide the time to remember what we humans have in common. Despite the enormity of pandemic pain and sorrow, some hoped it could provide a pivot point for humankind. Historically, a crisis can catalyze significant positive change—spiritual awakenings, the Renaissance, and others. On a personal level, perhaps it can inspire us to be more grateful and kind and remember to tell our families how much we love them.

Life is short. Life is precious.

Greater Iowa Youth for Christ staff members were fundraising to meet a growing need for youth programs in other parts of the state. But then the pandemic hit. "We are living at a unique time in history," executive director Derek Jacobsen wrote in an appeal letter. "COVID-19 has disrupted the entire world, and we are all trying to figure out how to navigate our way through it. We face a viral enemy that is invisible and extremely contagious. It spreads from person to person without us even knowing.

"But that's not the only thing that is contagious in our culture right now. So are fear, worry, and despair. The truth is, we are all carriers—not necessarily of the virus, but we each carry something. When we carry fear, we pass it on to others. When we carry worry, we spread it to those around us. When we carry doubt, we infect people without knowing it.

"Faith, Love and Hope … that's what we get to carry to these kids every day. We are carriers of faith and not fear, love and not rejection, hope and not despair. We are carriers of good news! We have determined that we will live by faith and not fear, we will shine the light and not hide it, we will be sacrificial and not selfish."

Perhaps this invisible enemy can show us that despite our differences, we are all interconnected. None of us operates in a vacuum. Dr. Martin Luther King Jr. referred to the interrelatedness of our actions in his famous "Letter from a Birmingham Jail," written on April 16, 1963.

As the coronavirus and its variants pass into history, can we say that we were our better selves?

Vaccines help provide the physical answer to a pandemic. But isn't the final cure a more fundamental change for our hearts?

> He has shown you, O mortal, what is good.
> And what does the Lord require of you?
> To act justly and to love mercy
> And to walk humbly with your God. (Micah 6:8 NIV)

God's Love

Amid this cacophony, let us pause and listen for the still, small voice.

For the gentle knock on the door from one who patiently waits for us to respond. The one who offers everlasting love and forgiveness, despite our stiff-necked obstinance and unwillingness to learn and get it right.

We read in the Bible to love God first and foremost. And Jesus told us to love one another, even difficult people, even our "enemies." Earnestly pray for them. Ask for God's grace to move toward them and encourage them instead of avoiding them. Look in that mirror as a reminder that any of us can sometimes be challenging.

> God is love. Whoever lives in love lives in God, and God in him. In this way, love is made complete ... And He has given us this command: Whoever loves God must also love his brother. (1 John 4:16–18, 21)

Sure, many of us have read so many verses, heard so many sermons, and read so many books about loving one another, about God's love.

But there are times when we can experience it.

Messengers

Maybe it happens when we finally surrender our battle to control the uncontrollable. Perhaps it is in those times when we feel the sheer agony of helplessly watching a loved one suffer as cancer metastasizes in her bones.

The Celtic Christians called it "Thin Places," physical places in which God's presence was more accessible, where boundaries between heaven and earth seemed to disappear.

I deeply wrestled with telling others about my life-changing experiences depicting God's love. I told Sue and a few family members. They all listened intently and said that the story gave them hope. After my mom passed on, I found several of her notes with "It's God's love" and other notes about the stories. That experience was a lifeline to get me through what happened with my sister. Then I remembered that several biblical stories featured birds as signs of hope.

So, I ventured to tell a few good friends, hoping they wouldn't think I was off my rocker, as I said to them that a bird-shaped cloud reminded me of who is with us in good times and bad. One friend reminded me that God provided a pillar of a cloud to help guide Moses and the Israelites out of Egypt. In those safe spaces of trust, friends said the stories helped them feel calmed and reassured. And many of them shared their own experiences.

A friend shared a story about the time she and her two sisters had with their mom, who was in the final stages of terminal breast cancer. Their mom told her daughters that she wanted to remind them of her love even after she was gone. She suddenly noticed a beautiful cardinal outside the window and suggested that her daughters could think of her whenever they saw a cardinal. So on the day she passed away, the daughters saw a beautiful cardinal outside her window that stayed for the entire day. And at difficult or sad times for their family, a cardinal inevitably makes an appearance.

And there was a friend whose dad loved goldfinches. Unfortunately, his elderly dad became quite ill and passed away after several months of loving caregiving by the family. After the funeral, when friends and family had gone, this friend was reluctant to return to the family house. But there, perched by the front door, was a goldfinch. Goldfinches were usually long gone at this time of the year because they migrated south to warmer temperatures.

Or there was the friend who saw a mourning dove for days outside her kitchen window after a dear friend died from cancer. Later, when her grandma died, two mourning doves became companions at their house. Her aunt died the night of her grandma's funeral; the next day, there were three doves. She continued to see the three doves for a long time.

And more recently, one of her good friends died in a tragic accident at work. She saw one mourning dove back at the house, which stayed there for days.

A bird provided hope for a prisoner who faced unimaginable loss and suffering in a Nazi concentration camp. Viktor Frankl was in agony when soldiers separated him from his wife after imprisoning them at the Auschwitz concentration camp. In his book, *A Man's Search for Meaning* (Viktor Frankl, Verlag fur Jugend und Volk, 1946), he wrote about how he had been persistently thinking about her, worried that she had died. Then, he suddenly deeply felt her presence. His wife's presence became even more tangible as a bird flew down, perched right in front of him, and looked steadily at him. Its timely presence instilled hope in him that helped him survive the death camp.

The World Food Prize Foundation president told a story of seeing an image of a dove before having a private audience with Pope Francis. And numerous other similar stories have been published or shared.

So, acknowledging that some may be skeptical, I'll share my bird messenger experiences about God's love:

Sue was still reeling from her devastating stage 4 breast cancer diagnosis when she read that Dr. Joan Borysenko would conduct a workshop in Madison. Borysenko was an instructor at Harvard Medical School and had written a *New York Times* best seller, *Minding the Body, Mending the Mind*, which Sue had read. Borysenko had the science pedigree—a doctorate in medical sciences from Harvard—and the real-life experience of losing her father to cancer. We registered for her workshop right away.

It was refreshing to hear her message about integrative medicine, the impact of our minds on our health, and the need for medical professionals to consider the patient as a spiritual whole. Major medical institutions were starting to explore complementary practices for pain management.

There is a basic human need for connection and healing, Borysenko said. It spans the globe and transverses cultural and language differences. She then led the several hundred participants in prayers. At the conclusion, a respectful silence enveloped us all.

Part of that basic need is for a physical connection. In our antiseptic and high-tech world, we often forget the healing that can come from a simple human touch of a friend or loved one. So we paired up and took turns massaging our partners' backs as calming music played. I was a bit skeptical. *But if nothing else, I can help Sue relax a bit with a backrub,* I thought.

I closed my eyes. I mentally repeated, *I hope for physical and spiritual healing for my Sue.* As I rubbed my sister's back, I visualized moving cancer down her spine and out of her body. It became a prayer of *Please, dear Lord, take this cancer away.* Down and out. Down and out.

And suddenly, it was as though the tumor took on wings and flew away like a bird. *That is odd. Maybe it symbolizes something. Perhaps an eagle?* I thought about eagle references in the Bible— about how those who hope in the Lord will renew their strength. Then, as we exchanged places with our partners, I excitedly told Sue about the image of the bird. She, too, thought it was beautiful and hopeful. We were so glad to be there together.

Too soon, the workshop was over, and it was time to go home. The sun was setting as I drove away from Madison, past the gently rolling Baraboo hills, one of Sue's favorite places. I glanced at the sunset and noticed this magnificent cloud. I thanked God for the beauty of this world and for the time to be with Sue.

I glanced again at the sunset before it disappeared. Hmm. The one cloud in the sky looked like it was in the shape of something, maybe a bird. I kept rubbernecking and struggling to stay on the interstate highway. Finally, I pulled over onto the shoulder and stopped the car. Whoa! *That is the shape of a bird. There are the wings, the head, and the beak. It is soaring.* And then it melted away into the sunset.

A bird? An eagle, maybe. It looked like the image of the bird I had seen earlier flying away from Sue.

Maybe a miracle is on its way for our Sue. I headed home, pondering what I had just seen.

I treasured that scene in my heart and regularly scanned the skies for another sighting. But it didn't happen.

A few years later, Sue's cancer had spread, and she had become mostly confined to her bed. I ran some errands for Sue, parked my car at the top of her long, winding driveway, and walked past the lovely patch of woods that hugged their house.

Deeply absorbed in thought about Sue, I headed toward the front door with grocery bags in hand when I noticed something out of the corner of my eye. Suddenly, three hawks came barreling out of her woods toward me. Before I could catch my breath, they were skyward, kettling higher and higher, riding the thermals in a dancing spiral. It was magnificent. I was transfixed. Higher and higher, they spiraled in their aerial waltz.

I had never seen anything like it. Higher and higher. I wanted to tell others to come to watch. But I couldn't move. I couldn't take my eyes off this astounding scene.

Then suddenly, one flew away from the other two. The two continued kettling straight upward. The third hawk that had separated from the others soared higher and higher in the other direction. And then it disappeared from my sight.

I am one of three sisters. Could one sister be soaring to places unseen?

I went inside. I couldn't tell anyone. I especially couldn't tell Sue what I had just seen. Not now. I held it close to my heart to share another day—maybe. But I wrote it all down when it happened so that I would not second-guess my memory.

A few months later, the final piece to this puzzle of bird and cloud experiences appeared. Sue and I talked one evening after she had a hard day recalling some bad experiences. I wanted to comfort her; I wanted those experiences never to have happened. I later headed to bed, where I prayed, tossed and turned, and eventually headed downstairs to a dark living room.

Following is part of the letter I wrote to Sue about this unforgettable experience. I first reminded Sue about the conference in Madison when I intensely pleaded for healing for my sister.

> When I concluded my pleas, I could sense the image of a bird soaring away. As I drove home from Madison that weekend, I noticed an unusual cloud formation in the sky as the sun began to set. It looked like a huge bird in the sky—the same as the one I saw at the meeting. It seemed to exude a sense of "freedom" or "peace." I had this strong feeling it meant Susie is free. I knew it was something very important and told you about this, not fully understanding it.
>
> I've tried to "wish" to see things in the clouds again, and it does not happen.
>
> The next time I saw the bird figure was the weekend you and Kevin were in Clear Lake in October. After you two left, there was the most incredible bird figure I had ever seen at sunset that night. I called to Tom to look at it. We even took a picture. And I thought again, it symbolizes something important for Sue and for all of us.
>
> You told me today about feeling vulnerable lately, of being susceptible to someone thinking

bad thoughts about you. You clearly were feeling fearful and also some anger over how our parents sometimes treated us. I wish we all had grown up with a sense of self-worth. I wish it had been easier and different. My heart feels broken and aches for you and all of us.

But we can't change the past. As you said, I think Mom wants to be a good mom and that Dad wants to be a good dad. They were doing the best they could at that time. We all can say and do things when we are frustrated that we don't mean, and too often, our loved ones bear the brunt. It seems like forgiveness is core to our very existence. Everyone has to forgive someone for something; some things are bigger than others. Yours are huge, and my heart aches about that.

Later, we all went to bed, but I could not sleep and headed downstairs. I was thinking how it must be so scary for you, and I wanted to do something or say something to help. But I wasn't sure what to do.

Maybe I remembered what it was like to be that vulnerable little kid. I was fearful, too, but I wanted to comfort and protect you. I felt so helpless.

What am I supposed to do? I'm so scared.

So, I started praying, fervently praying. I can't do this alone. I got on my knees. Dear sweet Jesus. Dear sweet Jesus. Please be with my sister. Please be with us all, dear Lord. Dear sweet Jesus, please be with us. Please. Dear sweet Jesus. Over and over.

I needed to let Duke [our dog] outside before heading upstairs. Stepping into the porch, I noticed the moon. It was gorgeous. It was icy cold, but I wanted to see it and hear the wind. So, I stepped outside on the deck and looked at the moon. There were just a few clouds right then by the moon. As I watched, a picture-perfect bird formed directly over the moon. I looked and listened to the winter wind. It stayed there for a few more seconds, although it seemed frozen in time. And then it was gone. But this time, I didn't stand there trying to interpret it. It was like a voice telling me—It's Love, God's Love, it is God's Love—over and over. And then it was like someone said in a good-natured way, "Do you finally get it? The bird is a dove, it shows God's love. Do you finally get it?" And then chuckling good-naturedly.

And I went inside with this "God's Love" in my head, hearing it over and over as I headed upstairs and then as I said my prayers. And I woke up the following day hearing God's Love, God's Love. It felt like it was washing over me, as though I was lying on a sandy, warm beach, and a blanket of warm ocean water lapped over me. I felt embraced. I remember thinking this sort of love is greater than any parent can ever have, even when one is in the mother-bear mode. Our earthly parents will always fall short, but tremendous love is available to us. God is our true parent. God weeps over our pain but is there to embrace us. God's love, God's love, God's love, love, love, love.

I started crying while trying to get ready that morning, and Tom came in, so I tried to tell him what had happened. He listened and said it was very important.

I knew I wanted to write this to you because it seemed important to share. It reminded me of part of the Whole Child/Whole Parent book I like so much. There's a section where it states, "...Our children are not our children. We are neither parents of our children nor children of our parents. We are all God's children and to the extent that we are nourished in this truth will our lives be reformed and transformed."

I'm not entirely sure what it all means. But I know I felt more strongly rooted, safer, and more at peace.

May God's love surround you and embrace you. God's love. Love.

Jan

God's love will get us through. God's love will endure.

Marsha and Her Final Gift

Marsha was one of the first friends that I told about these bird messenger stories. She listened. She didn't judge me or say that I had lost my marbles. Neither one of us completely understood the stories. Instead, we pondered and treasured them together.

Marsha was that kind of friend. I clearly remember when I met her years ago. She was someone I immediately knew I would enjoy. Of course, it helped that she loved to water-ski and did fun outdoor activities we both liked. But she also had a good sense of humor, wanted to learn new things, enjoyed people, didn't care for drama, and looked for the good in people and circumstances.

She loved to celebrate life's events like birthdays and holidays. But she didn't even need an occasion; she gathered people together with her gracious gift of hospitality and fabulous cooking. One of Marsha's favorite trademarks was to cut out photos she had taken of fun get-togethers during the year and tape them inside birthday cards. And she always ensured the card would arrive on or before the recipient's birthday, unlike *someone* who wasn't so great in her timeliness.

She and Barry adopted Rebecca a few years before our son was born, and we learned parenting tips from them. We had lots of fun as Rebecca and our son grew up with St. Patrick's Day treasure hunts, picnics in the woods, and boat rides on the lake. We loved that each of us was starting the day by telling our children, "This is the day the Lord has made; let us rejoice in it and be glad in it." Marsha innocently encouraged our son, Chris, to check out the litter of adorable puppies from the Humane Society. Yes, we did adopt a puppy.

We traveled together as couples to fun destinations with some outdoor adventure, whether it was snorkeling or taking a spur-of-the-moment, thirty-minute scuba diving lesson at the resort so we could check out a sunken ship.

Marsha and I had a pact that we would water-ski until we were sixty-five. Full transparency, however, we did change it to age sixty as we moved on in years. She was one of the coconspirators who sipped on wine and lit candles —both verboten, of course—to celebrate a birthday in a library study room. She thought it was fitting to give me a birthday card that said, "You are only young once, but you can stay immature indefinitely."

She traveled with me to help remove items at my recently deceased cousin's apartment on posh Fifth Avenue in New York City. We had hoped to see a Broadway play and eat at some unique restaurants. But instead, we spent most of our time in a frenzy trying to load furniture and clothes into a small sedan during rush hour traffic in downtown Manhattan. She was a great sport and chalked it all up to one of life's exciting adventures.

She hung in there when I carried on grieving about Sue.

To me, Marsha embodied the fruits of the Spirit.

She never claimed a holier-than-thou position, but she had this high-gear drive to serve others as she sought God's will. Not that she was perfect; none of us are. But she was mighty close. Countless organizations benefitted from her behind-the-scenes volunteer projects and her professional work. She measurably improved life in numerous small towns by obtaining funding to rebuild aging water and sanitary treatment facilities. She was bright and a quick study.

We assumed there would be more travel adventures and fun on the lake.

But then Marsha's hip started bothering her. By the time doctors figured it out, it was stage 4 leiomyosarcoma (LMS) cancer, rare cancer for which there is no cure.

There was shock, disbelief, and anger that doctors did not diagnose cancer earlier.

Then she and Barry had a "no regrets" conversation. They concluded that they would only look forward and live the time remaining to the fullest.

A particularly hideous and aggressive cancer, LMS starts in the smooth muscles that line organs. In Marsha's case, it was her uterus. She had surgeries and chemo. She focused on being grateful that she could tolerate the chemo. She celebrated when she could ride her bike around the lake again. This former high school basketball and golf athlete prioritized keeping on moving. She didn't complain. She just dealt with it.

She regularly read devotionals, including one that I had given her. She said her favorite one focused on following Jesus one step at a time, walking by faith, and focusing on the present instead of the mountains ahead.

Family and friends across the country kept praying for miracles and more precious time. But the pain and discomfort were growing.

Too soon, doctors said there was nothing more they could do.

She was admitted to hospice and encircled by the prayers of many. A beautiful sunset that evening reminded me of Marsha's countless sunset photos. She could see the uniqueness in each.

Marsha had created a final gift for us all, spreading hope and love in her memorial service. Hundreds of people packed into the legendary Surf Ballroom, one of Marsha and Barry's favorite gathering places. As we looked at the people of all ages in that ballroom, it was clear that this remarkable woman had touched many lives. Maybe it was her kindness and her zest for life, or perhaps it was because she would listen to you like you were the only one in the room. "And we thought *we* were her best friends," a friend and I tried to say with a smile at the service.

The song "No Longer Slaves" set the tone. "I'm no longer a slave to fear; I am a child of God."

Pastor Brad Thornton was one of the pastors at the service. "Marsha was a person who found guidance and comfort in the scriptures," he said, noting that she had favorite verses that she wanted to be the basis of her funeral service. "One was in Philippians 4, where Paul says, 'Rejoice. Again, I say rejoice. Let your kindness be known to all.' Another came from 1 Thessalonians 5: 'Rejoice always. Give thanks in all circumstances, for this is the will of God for you.' But the one I think forms the basis of her story and the essence of who she was is found in Romans 12, 1–2, which says,

> I appeal to you, brothers and sisters, by the mercies of God to present your bodies as a living sacrifice to God, *which is your reasonable service.* Do not be conformed to this world but be transformed by the renewing of your minds, so that you may discern what is the will of God—what is good and acceptable and perfect.

"She gave of herself in service and as long as no one knew or gave her praise for it, she was just fine, because that was, in her mind, her reasonable service. But there's another part of Marsha that is tied up in the Romans passage. And that has to do with discerning the will of God.

"You see, Marsha had a deep sense of the holy. She had a deep connection with the things of God. Her passion was always to discern the will of God for her life. She felt led, oftentimes. And she could be grieved that she might not have understood God's will. That was one of the big question marks of her life these past months and years. Did I misread the will of God? Did I not discern where God wanted me to be and to do? It wasn't so much that this thing had happened to her. It was whether she had made the right decisions leading up to it; whether she had misread what it was that God was telling her and leading her.

"She wrestled with that, and I think came to some sort of peace with it when people from all parts of her life began to send her the same Bible verse. It vexed her at first, I think because she told me one time, 'whenever I open up an email, it's the same verse. This morning when I opened up my devotion book, there it was.' It was the verse from the Psalm 46 that says. 'Be still and know that I am God.' Now that is not an easy thing for someone with a type-A personality to do. It wasn't easy for Marsha, either. But as I remembered things this week, I remembered something I heard both Marsha and Barry say several times this past year: 'God has a plan. We don't know what it is. But God has a plan.'

"She was passionate about serving and discerning the will of God; and she was passionate about her family, too. She and Barry were a true love story. We saw that all the time. In the obituary that she wrote for herself, she said how much she always appreciated his patience and understanding. That appreciation was a two-way street. I will never forget Barry saying one time how lucky he felt that a guy like him could have been the one to have married Marsha. She loved her daughter Rebecca and treasured the times they were together. She would always tell us about Rebecca's life and her adventures with a tone and a look of fierce pride."

Pastor Thornton joked about Marsha not wanting to be in the limelight; she didn't want anyone to know everything she did at church behind the scenes. But Pastor Thornton was glad he could finally spill the beans about her generosity that touched so many.

"So, I've tried to tell the truth on her as best I could. But she would want me to tell you the whole truth. And that is this: That she did all of what she did in life only because of the grace of God. You see, Christianity is a resurrection religion. We believe in resurrection. Without resurrection, our faith means nothing. But resurrection isn't something that happens someday far away, on the last day. Resurrection happens here, every day. The New Testament is clear about that. Paul referred to his life as being buried with Christ in baptism and being raised to walk in a new life, a new way. We participate in Christ's resurrection in the way we put to death the bias and the hatreds that separate us from one another and from God. In resurrection we become a new creation, not because we are good or have worked hard enough to have made ourselves that way. We participate in resurrection because of the life, death, and resurrection of Jesus Christ. We can come to love God because God first loved us. Marsha believed that. It formed the basis of who she was and who she wanted to be. She presented herself to God because when you've been raised with Christ, it is your reasonable service.

"And in that faith and belief, she sought to live out the words of Jesus that whoever would be greatest among you must be your servant and the servant of all will be the greatest of all."

Marsha had written a message, which was read out loud to everyone:

> To every single person who mailed a card or typed an email or delivered food or gave a prayer or texted a message or sent flowers or picked out an inspirational gift—I cannot tell you how much your kindness was valued. I appreciated

every effort made on my behalf and sometimes was astounded when I would read the heartfelt thoughts that many of you expressed. The messages were so touching and so profound and so loving and so absolutely raw in emotions being expressed that I felt truly humbled to have such wonderful support being sent my way.

I hope that all of you will continue those efforts of kindness to support others in need. You may not always understand how important those efforts are. Now you know. Keep it up. Nothing beats showing love to others.

During the last seven to eight years of my life, I have reflected a lot and tried to pinpoint what it is that makes my life here on earth so happy. I guess it isn't any one thing. It can't be pinned on just having a career that I loved. Or a daughter that is the light of my life. Or a patient and understanding husband. Or caring and wonderful brothers, far-away cousins, and family members. Or my deep and personal relationship with God and the Holy Spirit who lives within me. Or living in a wonderful place like Clear Lake.

There is a quote attributed to Helen Keller that reads, "My friends have made the story of my life." I had never really thought in those terms, but I agree with the sentiment. I think what has made my life so meaningful is the relationships that have developed with friends over my lifetime. Some of the relationships are long-term, forever, since childhood. Some of them are relatively new.

For those of you lucky enough to live in the same town or area as your family, I envy you. I didn't have that. My family members are very spread out and so having birthday get-togethers wasn't possible ... The distance from family members makes my relationships with friends all the more important.

The circumstances and backgrounds of those that intersected my life are varied, but as I reflected, I began to appreciate the good fortune of knowing them. We never know who might enter our life or when. We do not know what the journey from any one point in life to another will look like, or who we will encounter along the way ... For me it was card club members, wine club members, church friends, neighborhood friends, childhood friends, high school friends, college friends, those friends I worked with, golf friends, friends I met through Rebecca's schoolmates, and random Clear Lake people that I have gotten to know over the years. Taken together, these relationships changed me as a person and influenced the direction of my life.

The fact that each relationship was so different and carried me in different ways made life full and interesting and added up to a wonderful balance of fun, inspiration, deep faith, serious conversations, annual traditions, fellowship, love, great food, enlightenment, moonlit boat rides, Ferris wheel rides, trombone concerts, beautiful sunsets, and tasty gin and tonics.

While not everything in my life was exactly how I thought it would be, on the balance, my sixty-four years were many, many times beyond my best hopes. I'm sure that most people I know have things in their lives that they wish different. But most of us are so lucky to be where we are that we should thank God and our family members and our friends at any opportunity that we have.

I am now at a point where I am really glad to have awakened to what is going on around me and to appreciate what I have and to thank God every single day to be so blessed. I truly feel that my life was better because of this awakening. I see more things, notice things I didn't before, and feel that when I do die, I won't have as many regrets or have a "wish I would have done things differently" kind of attitude.

I hope that others who are my friends have either found this kind of contentment or will someday have a similar renaissance. It isn't something someone can lead you into. It is a very private, on-your-own kind of tradition ...

In summary, thanks for being part of my life. You were all a part of my community, and without your touch and support, my life would not have been as rich. I have been blessed. Peace, love, and gratitude to you. —M.

As Pastor Thornton said, "Well done thou good and faithful servant; enter into the joys of your Lord." Amen.

Godspeed, my dear friend.

Maren

Maren, age twenty-seven and mother of two young children, left a timeless message for her loving family. Maren had a genetic condition called neurofibromatosis. This disease typically causes benign tumors to grow in the body, but Maren sadly was among the small percentage that developed malignant tumors. Cancer in her hip caused doctors to remove her left leg and pelvis. Doctors thought they had completely removed the tumor, but it had spread to her brain and bones.

Her family was at her bedside in hospice as she slept. She suddenly awoke and said to seven of her loved ones in the room, "I had this dream … somebody told me that the play was starting, and I should get ready to say my lines. I said, 'But I don't know my lines.' He said, 'That is okay. Just say what is in your heart.'"

Then Maren began her prayer:

> God bless everybody in this room … and all the people who have been praying for me. I know that God is with me now and will be with me when I enter heaven. I know He loves me. If I can't walk, He will carry me. He will never give me more pain than I can handle. I ask forgiveness for my sins. I know Jesus died on the cross to save me from sins. I pray for all the ministers and clergy and rabbis who stand in the pulpit and preach God's love. You know you can even be a person on the street and just stop somebody and tell them about God's love. I want everybody to know that God loves you and He is always near, and you can call on Him.

Then she fell asleep.

The pastor shared Maren's words at her funeral service, and her mom, Kathy, hoped her daughter's positive message would touch others. Maren's comment, "If I can't walk, He will carry me," was especially poignant since doctors removed her leg and pelvis.

Kathy, a longtime friend, shared her daughter's positive message with others including mutual friend Marsha, about two months before Marsha passed away. Marsha's email response was the following:

Wow. That is powerful. You are lucky that your sister wrote this all down. Such clarity in her prayer ... at a time when she had to have been weak and tired and confused.

When I am weak, then I am strong.

Her message is consistent with devotions I have been reading lately. I have noticed that so many of them (despite being from a variety of sources) have the very central message of Love One Another. That the only thing that really matters is to Love others. Simple.

Thanks for sharing.

M.

Kathy shared another message of comfort forged out of tragic loss. Her thirty-five-year-old brother, Phil, was killed in 1981 in a plane crash in Africa while working for the State Department. He left behind his young wife and a ten-month-old son. Kathy's family was devastated. "How does one recover from a tragedy so sudden and, to us who were left, with no good reasons for this to happen?" she said. Kathy's father was a Lutheran church pastor, but the previous church pastor and good friend, Dr. Al Rogness, conducted the service. Dr. Rogness's twenty-two-year-old son had been killed in a traffic accident years before, so he could intimately share their grief on the sudden loss of a child and brother.

Kathy emphasized that to this day, decades later, the words from the pastor's service have helped with her loss of loved ones. Here are parts of Dr. Rogness's sermon:

There are lessons to be learned; if not learned, at least they are reminders at this hour. In the first place, did you ever know that you loved this much? If we understood how much we love each

221

other in a family and out beyond the family to friends, if we understood and felt the depth and the intensity of that love while the commonplace of life goes on, we couldn't stand it. But we do have far greater love for each other than we know, and occasions like this where we face the loss reminds us of that, and we better remember that those who are left and those who are near us are as dear to us as our lost one.

Another thing death does for us, is that we begin to deal with memories. Now many memories are good, and some memories aren't good. Some memories are filled with regrets and remorse and guilt. But what are we going to do with those? There is only one place to put them and that is at the foot of the Cross. Package them and put them there. If ever you have regrets, you wish you had done this or you had failed to do this, or you wished you hadn't done this, so you live with that. What are you going to do with that? You just can't grovel in death, and the reason you mustn't is that you have a right to put that in the sweeping forgiveness of our Lord Jesus Christ.

At the moment that I was able to drop grief after our son Paul's death, I found myself thinking, "I can't drop grief, I can't stop grieving, because if I stop grieving, that is evidence that I didn't love him after all." So it almost became a duty to grieve. And then a strange thing happened. I pictured Paul in the bleachers now cheering me on when I dropped grief and saying, "Dad, you're making it!" to return to the common life with joy in this, however I was able. Not always

was I able, or am I able, but at least I have a
mandate from the bleachers who are cheering
me on. And I think I have always wondered how
thin the veil is between those of us who are left
and those who are there. And at my age, I've got
quite a company on the other side of friends and
members of the family, and I like to think of them
in the bleachers, cheering us on.

Kathy said Dr. Rogness told family and friends that "death
reminds us that we really don't belong to each other. We are
loaned to one another for a few swift years here. But we are loaned
to one another, to care for and love one another. We belong only
to Him who created us and redeemed us and has made Himself
a part of us. And it is a remarkable privilege to have the right to
care for and love one another."

"I think it is an interesting thought to say we are loaned to
one another," Kathy said. "The verb 'loaned' implies immediacy,
whereas 'belong' implies forever. We need to realize that we need
to show love and caring each day on this earth because we don't
have forever."

Open the Door

My husband, son, and I were excited to see the beautiful
architecture, collections, and artwork in the venerable St. Paul's
Cathedral in London. We enthusiastically made our way around
the cathedral floor and other areas. Then, we passed through a
doorway into a chapel and stood speechless—in front of us was
The Light of the World painting. My husband, son, and I stood
transfixed and teary-eyed to see it firsthand.

When Jesus spoke again to the people, he said, "I
am the light of the world. Whoever follows me

will never walk in darkness, but will have the light of life." (John 8:12 NIV)

Artist Holman Hunt shook the artistic world in 1854 with his depiction of the book of Revelation 3:20 and John 8:12, "I am the light of the world." "Apparently, Holman Hunt intended to show Jesus standing outside the door to the individual's heart," wrote Dr. Eric Hayden in his "Light of the World" booklet available at the cathedral. "The door may never have been opened. The doorway is overgrown with weeds, and there is no handle visible. As a consequence, Jesus can knock, but it is up to the individual to open the door and to trust 'The Light of the World' with His symbolic lantern to guide him or her through the darkness of the world outside."

> Here I am! I stand at the door and knock. If anyone hears my voice and opens the door, I will come in and eat with him and he with me. (Revelation 3:20 NIV)

A Work in Progress

Intellectually, we know that painful experiences are inevitable at some time in our life. But still, life can be so gut-wrenching when our loved ones are in agony. Or when they leave us. Does my heart still ache for Sue? Of course. There are often gentle nudges when I think *Sue would have enjoyed that*. And there are other times when I want to kneel on the floor and call out, "Susie!" as I did helplessly as the hearse pulled away. And then weep. And weep.

The miracle of Sue's physical healing didn't happen. Dad survived the war in Korea but succumbed to Alzheimer's. Mom had to watch her daughter die. Children and families are torn apart by war; teenagers can do desperate acts; spouses can abuse; diseases can ravage our bodies. So how do we keep our hearts from hardening through life's pain and disappointments? Wise men and women throughout the ages have cautioned us that a hardened heart is more toxic than any disease.

It is a choice. We have free will in this lifelong journey. Mary, Craig, Hedi, Mary Ann, Sue, Fred, Char, and others didn't choose their circumstances. But as painful and challenging as they were, they decided how to react. "We can't choose what will happen to us next month or next week," Pastor Harlan said. "But you can choose how you will respond, whether it will make you or break you, whether you will be a bitter or better person."

Yet, despite what I have learned, I am such a work in progress. I fall so far short each day in my thoughts, actions, and inactions. I even need reminders that I am never alone in getting through this storm. It is comforting to remember that even the disciples needed reassurance, as noted in the *Jesus calms the storm* scripture:

> One day Jesus said to his disciples, "Let's go over to the other side of this lake." So they got into a boat and set out. As they sailed, he fell asleep. A squall came down on the lake, so that the boat was being swamped, and they were in great danger.
>
> The disciples went and woke him, saying "Master, Master, we're going to drown!"
>
> He got up and rebuked the wind and the raging waters; the storm subsided, and all was calm. "Where is your faith?" He asked His disciples.
>
> In fear and amazement, they asked one another, "Who is this? He commands even the winds and the water, and they obey him." (Luke 8: 22–25 NIV)

I give thanks for Your patience when I sometimes still try to steer the ship, to white-knuckle it when I'm feeling needy and vulnerable. Please help me to remember to be still and calm, to slide over in the lifeboat to make room for the Captain. Thank You for helping me understand that Your healing includes broken hearts and relationships, not always physical healing. Thank You for being willing to walk alongside us each day, through the joys and the sorrows, each moment, each hour, each day. I am forever thankful.

> You turned my wailing into dancing;
> You removed my sackcloth and clothed me with joy, that my heart may sing to you and not be silent.
> Oh Lord my God, I will give you thanks forever.
> (Psalm 30:11–12 NIV)

Through these shared stories and life experiences, we can see that our purpose is not to reach a stagnant point of achieving a title or status when we are "grown-up." But it is an ongoing process, as Mother Teresa wrote:

> We must know that we have been created for greater things, not just to be a number in the world, not just to go for diplomas and degrees, this work and that work. We have been created in order to love and be loved. (Mother Teresa, *Where There is Love, There is God: A Path to Closer Union with God and Greater Love for Others*, Doubleday, 2010)

Our loving God provides hope through the pain. But it is a process, not an instant solution like we want in our immediate gratification society. Pastor Harlan said it is part of God's goal to develop a more spiritually mature character in each of us.

The Core

I am grateful that we all can be renewed and rebuilt and that we can continuously become a better version of ourselves *as* we grow up. It all starts with the core, with God's love. Our hearts radiate that love as we grow in a deeper relationship. Our My Better Self actions emanate from Your unfailing light and love. It is a way of showing gratitude for how You first loved us.

"We were made with a God-shaped vacuum in our lives, and when you try to fill that with anything else, it's like trying to put a square peg into a round hole. It doesn't fit," Pastor Harlan said. "God made you to know Him. He made you for a reason. The starting point of that purpose is to understand that He made you for a relationship. And when we deepen your relationship with Him, there is a sense of peace that comes into your life."

> Peace I leave with you; my peace I give you. I do not give to you as the world gives. Do not let your hearts be troubled and do not be afraid. (John 14: 25–27 NIV)

> My command is this: Love one another as I have loved you. (John 15:12 NIV)

In the uncertainty of an ever-changing world, amid any internal fears and outward storms we encounter, there is certainty. It is God's love that carries us through and sets us free. With gratefulness and still astonishment at Your unfailing Love, I will never forget,

"Do you get it? It is God's love."

About the Author

Jan Lovell, M.S., is an award-winning former journalist and current business owner who was a staff writer and editor for newspapers in Oregon, Minnesota, and Iowa and has published numerous freelance articles. As a sister, wife, mother, and grandmother, she hopes this book will provide beacons along a reader's journey so we can act with more compassion, faith, joy, and love.